Intentional Influence

A Biblical Woman's Guide to Mentoring

Beth Bingaman

ISBN # 978-1-9876-9892-3

TABLE OF CONTENTS

Introduction

The first time a friend suggested to me that I had a "sphere of influence" I thought, "Who does she think I influence?" The puzzled look on my face caused her to explain. She encouraged me to think about my own children, the women who heard me answer questions in a Bible study, and the women I was working with who witnessed my responses to stressful situations. I had never thought about it. As I did, I could clearly see how others had influenced me. She gave me a new understanding that I could have an "intentional influence" or I could just roll along, not thinking about how what I say or do affects the people around me.

Though I attended church most of my life, I had very little Bible knowledge. In His grace, the Lord introduced me to Christian radio. Within a short time I understood the truth of Jesus Christ's death and resurrection as God's plan for my salvation. He provided a Christian friend who invited me to join a small group Bible study with several women I did not know. In that group I was influenced, taught, loved, and encouraged to grow in faith, knowledge, and understanding of the Lord. Looking back, I see how each of those women (some whose names I cannot remember) influenced my thinking as God was at work teaching me through them.

God's Preparation

Several years later, I was introduced to a Bible Study Fellowship class. I began as a student but God later called me to teach that class. After teaching for eight years, I left that ministry to teach in my local church and, as God gave opportunity, to speak and teach in other places such as retreats and women's ministry banquets.

One invitation I received was to speak at a church for a one-day retreat on mentoring. The retreat leaders named it "Intentional Friendships" because they wanted to encourage the women of their local assembly to build relationships with each other. I accepted the invitation and began to pray about what the Lord would have me say.

Considering mentoring in the context of friendship as well as discipleship, I was given to understand that what biblical mentors do,

1

as the retreat title pointed out, is intentional; it is thought out according to God's Word.

In mentoring relationships the mentor, quite intentionally, attempts to influence the mentee to think about things in a new or different way. When the mentoring (also known as discipling) relationship is between two Christian women, the goal of the intentional influence will be, as "iron sharpens iron," a more biblical outlook. These are relationships that grow as two women spend time together in true fellowship around God's Word.

Acts of service, love and encouragement are intentional toward those we mentor, just as they are towards those who are our family and friends. Mentoring opportunities are sometimes costly with respect to time, but they are important in building relationships that glorify God, grow His Kingdom, and help one another.

In preparation for the "Intentional Friendships" retreat, I dug further into what Scripture says about mentoring. How exciting to see the encouragement for Christian sisters to love, serve, and encourage one another and God's specific instructions regarding what topics older women are to teach younger women (Titus 2:3-5). The Bible confirmed what God had been teaching me through my experience with women in the church. Listing those I'd met with over the years (some I did not even realize I was "mentoring"), I was surprised by the number, but also by the relationships that developed as a result of spending time together, intentionally looking into God's Word.

Mentoring Experience

My experience with mentoring has come from different sources. A Pastor asked me to mentor some of them as new believers. Two came to me and asked because of problems at home. Another was sent to me by a mutual friend. She thought I would be able to help in a crisis situation the young woman was in, but did not want to discuss with her friends. You will read about them in this book. (I have their permission to share their stories though all of the names have been changed.) Some have had painful pasts. Some, like me, came to faith a little later in life and wanted more Bible knowledge. Each one, in her own unique way, was looking for someone to come alongside her to help her grow in her faith in Jesus Christ as she navigated life's challenges. Today, though I am not in close contact with many of them, they have special places in my heart as instruments God used in the process of my own sanctification and growth in faith.

Blessings Overflow

Mentoring provides the personal benefit (and challenge) of helping us see our own personalities and faith more clearly, giving us unique opportunities to work on our own holiness, while intentionally helping those we mentor. As a result, I have seen parts of me that had not been as obvious in friendships or work relationships. For instance, while I prefer to think of myself as assertive, I have learned that some women have found me to be blunt (ouch!). I'm also very concrete when it comes to the Bible. I love God's Word and understand that obedience is necessary to receive the blessings God promises. I have had to think intentionally about how to convey the Bible's practical truths to new believers who may see God's Word as more spiritual in nature. God refined my teaching skills in this process. Both the mentor and the mentee receive blessings in the relationship.

See, I am setting before you today a blessing and a curse: the blessing, if you obey the commandments of the LORD your God, which I command you today. Deuteronomy 11:26-28

God is faithful to keep His promises.

As mentors, we have the privilege of influencing the thinking of others so they may see what they might need to change to please God and improve their own lives. What I have learned over time, from working with women in difficult situations, is that some who have been hurt in life sometimes think they should receive blessings in return for the suffering, rather than for faith and obedience. This is not biblical thinking. (I suppose that may sound blunt.) Unbiblical ideas like these have to change in order to resolve problems in marriages, in raising children, in work relationships, and in order to live a life pleasing to God, which brings blessing. These truths have to be taught in a way that someone who has already been the victim of someone else, does not become the victim of an uncompassionate mentor or teacher. Godly mentoring will intentionally obey God's command to speak the truth in love.

We Work – God Changes

For the mentor, it is equally unbiblical to think that we can have a life-transforming influence on a person, a marriage, or any of the other circumstances in another person's life by our own knowledge or teaching. Only God, through the work of His Holy Spirit, changes things Godward. The influence we attempt to have needs to be biblical. Only the Holy Spirit can work in the other woman to bring His transformation in her thinking. Amazingly, He gives us opportunities to be His servants, bringing His truth to their attention.

God has many women in need of these truths. We never know how He will bring them to us, as they are both inside, and outside, of our local churches. If we deliberately look for ways to serve, and let others know we are willing, God will bring the opportunity.

Where do They Come From?

The first time I was approached it was by my Pastor. He asked me to come alongside of a new believer who had come into the church. Shortly after that, an acquaintance in our church came to me when we were serving together in the nursery and said she was in need of help. Her marriage was very difficult and she was looking for someone who could help her keep her eyes on the Lord as she tried to stay in the marriage and insist on change. As we looked together at God's Word, praised God when we saw Him at work, and pleaded with Him when she was afraid or discouraged, we worked to allow God's Word to be the biggest influence on her life and decisions. We'll hear more about this later.

One by one, as they learned I was willing, the Lord brought women to me with varying issues, looking for biblical counsel. Once people know you are willing to mentor, the opportunities seem to find you. In this book, I talk about ways to discern which ones are for you, and which ones to refer to others. You will also find practical teaching to assist you in helping other women find spiritual and emotional growth.

Biblical Influence

I consider myself an ordinary woman, happily married for thirty-eight years, the mother of two (now adult) children, and grandmother to four precious grandchildren. Our marriage and children have gone through the normal ups and downs of life on earth. We have had times of great joy, times of sorrow, good times and difficult times as our kids were growing up. One of our regrets is that we did not come to know the Lord until my husband and I were almost forty. This means our children did not get to see us model biblical thinking and living until they were pre-teens. A huge opportunity for biblical influence was lost in those years. I am praying that between us, we can help others to avoid that pitfall. If more women will mentor, more children will have a greater influence of biblical thinking in their lives.

Serving God – Influencing Generations

I hope that after reading this book you will be encouraged to come alongside a woman to mentor her--to influence her to grow in faith and understanding of what God can accomplish in and through her, when she consciously places full faith in Him. Mentoring is an intentional, time-consuming act on our part. It can be emotionally difficult. The blessing we receive may be God allowing us to see the godly influence the mentee is on others, especially the next generation of her own family.

As an added bonus, when you think about being intentional in all of your relationships, you may enjoy deeper bonds in them as a result of applying the biblical principles discussed in this book,

The Assumptions

Two assumptions underlie this book.

First, the Word of God is the law of life. The Bible is God's instruction manual. He gave it to us as a plumb line, a measure with which to compare our lives. When we obey His Word in faith and confidently trust Him to direct our paths, we will be blessed with the fruits of the Spirit: love, joy, peace, patience, kindness, gentleness, goodness, faithfulness, and self-control (Galatians 5.22-23). When we rebel against Him and His Word, we will not experience these fruits in our lives. His blessings and curses are directly related to obedience and are for His glory and our good.

The second assumption is that you (the reader) are a born-again Christian. We truly have nothing to offer in terms of mentoring another if we do not have the power of the Holy Spirit in us, teaching, directing our paths, and giving us wisdom. True change can only happen as God does the work. If He is not in us to work through us, we will waste our own time and the time of the one seeking a mentor. If you are not sure about your salvation, please put this book down now and seek the guidance of a trusted Christian friend or Pastor.

The Organization

The book is broken into three sections:

- The Mandate: Concentrating on God's expectations in His command for older Christian women to mentor younger Christian women
- The Methods: A view of different kinds of mentoring relationships as well as a Christian understanding of friendships.
- The Mentoring: Exploring God's instructions from Titus 2 and some practical "how-to's" of the mentoring process.

May God be magnified, the readers edified, and future generations intentionally influenced from a biblical perspective by the use of this book.

Beth Bingaman 2018

Section 1: The Mandate

2
An Intentional Investment

Oil and perfume make the heart glad, and the sweetness of a friend comes from his earnest counsel. Proverbs 27:9

She shows up when you feel down. She listens when you need to talk. She hears what you mean, not just your words. She talks when you only want to listen. She watches your kids when you need a break. She meets you for lunch so you can get away from the mess. She meets you for tea at home so you can stay in the mess. She "likes" your Facebook posts. She responds to your emails.

Sadly, for some women in today's culture, this kind of personal relationship is very difficult to develop. Women are busy with work, children, ministry, volunteer work, organizations, and the pressure to have children in multiple activities - sports, music, and drama - so they can get into the right college or be associated with the right group. The pressure is great on parents and children. For the wife, mother, employee, ministry leader, and taxi-driver, close friendships can take a back seat so that when a woman needs someone to help bear a burden or rejoice with her, there is no one to whom she can turn.

Getting "connected" to others takes many forms today, although the online connection is the channel most often used. This kind of connection includes the various social networks, playing computer games with others remotely located, or even studying the Word of God from the comfort of our own home in large on-line "communities." We "feel" connected but the reality is that our ability to interact with others is limited by our internet connection and a device with a screen. We miss out on a person's body language that tells us a lot about how well we are communicating with others, and we lose the ability to 'read' the other person. Sometimes it is not until a crisis hits that we realize that these 'connections' are not very "close," and the people in these "communities" are not really good friends.

There was a point in the early ministry of Jesus when His disciples returned after being out ministering on their own. They were tired but also wanted to talk with him and each other about their experiences.

Jesus invited them to come away with Him to a quiet place where they could rest, and talk, free from the throngs of people whose needs were so great that they had not even permitted Jesus and the disciples the leisure to eat. As they sailed away, the crowds, anticipating where the boat was headed, ran ahead on foot arriving before Jesus and His disciples.

Mark 6:34 describes how Jesus saw the crowd and had compassion on them, *because they were like sheep without a Shepherd.* He gave up His plan to get away to rest and began to teach them "many things." He and His disciples even fed this large crowd.

Compassion. Kindness. Giving up His own plan. Jesus was different from most of the people we meet. He showed compassion and made time for the crowd when it had not been in His plans to do so. With Jesus as our example of intentionally going to the people, we need to learn to intentionally invest time in personal contact - in person, not only on a screen - if we want to have meaningful, biblically-based relationships with women as friends or mentors.

The idea of being friends rather than mentors seems attractive to most of us. The word "mentoring" sounds so formal. The Oxford Dictionary definition of mentor is: "an experienced and trusted advisor." The act of mentoring is described as "to advise or train someone (especially a younger colleague)." The one I think best describes my experience of mentoring is from Webster's New World Dictionary: "a teacher or a coach."

On the other hand, friendship, is defined as a person attached to another by feelings of affection or personal regard. Another definition describes a friend as a person who gives assistance; a patron; a supporter: e.g. friends of the Boston Symphony.

One of the truths I hope you take away from this book is that if we will offer our time to mentor, we may come away, after a time, with the affection and personal regard for each other that can best be described as friendship. My experience is that there will be a blessing in it. God teaches us that when we obey His commands He will bless us. One of those blessings is the friendship that often develops out of our intentionality in mentoring relationships.

From my own observations, many Christian women would define mentoring as a formal, structured, sit down counseling session, usually with a Bible Study where the "trusted advisor" guides the conversation according to scriptural teaching. Indeed, this *is* one form of mentoring. To some, that sounds quite intimidating. Perhaps it sounds like too much work, or it insinuates that we must be studied and experienced enough to help someone else. Maybe it is the formal structure of a mentor relationship that causes discomfort. For some, the mere mention of mentoring seems to invoke an excuse posing as humility: *"Oh, I'm not spiritually mature enough to do that."* All of this keeps us from intentionally investing time and energy in the life of another.

This more formal kind of mentoring does indeed take preparation time, prayer time, and meeting time. It requires effort and commitment on the part of both the mentor and the one being mentored. In the Bible, words and phrases such as "disciple," "build one another up," "encourage one another," and "serve one another," are used to restate these expectations.

The Bible commands every parent to teach every child the Word and ways of God. Mentoring the next generation in our own households is included in the call. Though they are less "friendly" the commands are clear. Mentoring starts with "teach your children":

And these words that I command you today shall be on your heart. You shall teach them diligently to your children, and shall talk of them when you sit in your house, and when you walk by the way, and when you lie down, and when you rise. You shall bind them as a sign on your hand, and they shall be as frontlets between your eyes. You shall write them on the doorposts of your house and on your gates. Deuteronomy 6:6-9

The second command is for "older women to teach the younger women." It calls for older women to live a lifestyle of "teaching" and "training" younger women. The discipling of other, less mature sisters in the Lord, is a call of God for all women, and for every Christian:

Older women likewise are to be reverent in behavior, not slanderers or slaves to much wine. They are to teach what is good, and so train the young women to love their husbands and children, to be self-controlled, pure, working at home, kind, and submissive to their own husbands, that the Word of God may not be reviled. Titus 2:3-5

Our responsibility started at home, then expanded to other women, and now turns to the nations. The third command that is a big part of mentoring is to "go and make disciples." We are to go and make disciples who will teach others, with the help of the Holy Spirit, to observe the commands of God. In Matthew 28:19-20 Jesus said:

Go therefore and make disciples of all nations, baptizing them in the name of the Father and of the Son and of the Holy Spirit, teaching them to observe all that I have commanded you. And behold, I am with you always, to the end of the age. Matthew 28:19-20

From these verses we can see the commands we have as older women in the faith to minister to others: our children first, women in the church second, and then, to whomever the Lord sends us. In Romans 8:29, God states His predestined plan for us to be conformed to the image of Jesus Christ. As Christ lived and died for us, His purposes and plans were intentional. If we are to be conformed to His image, we too, must be intentional in how we relate to others.

Who, Me?

We are a people of excuses. We make excuses for doing, or not doing, all kinds of things in our lives. One of the challenges we face as Christians is to not excuse away the commands of God. A child of God is to be obedient to His commands (Deuteronomy 8:20; 11:27, John 14:15). The problem for many of us is that we read and understand the commands but find no clear directions in the Scriptures for how to carry them out. For instance, I know as a mother and grandmother I have a responsibility to pass on the truths of the Scripture to the next generation. The Bible does not get so specific about how to introduce children and grandchildren to the Word of God or what books to read to my grandchildren or which ones to avoid. I, personally, need enough knowledge of the Word of God and the leading of the Holy Spirit to discern the details for myself.

As an "older woman" I have a responsibility to teach and train the younger women of the body of Christ. The Scriptures do not clearly define "older" and "younger" or what "teaching and training" will look like. Older may be older in the faith or it may also mean older in age. I once recommended a woman to mentor who was at least ten years younger than the woman wanting help. The younger woman had a lot of experience with the issues the older woman was facing and had been studying the scriptures for much longer.

Teaching and training can look different depending on the need, and the women involved. We may hold a bible study in our own home with several women at once, or be intentional about talking to younger women on Sunday mornings before we leave church. A long-term one-on-one relationship with a young woman assigned by our pastor may be how the relationship begins, or someone else may only need a one-time opportunity to chat and ask questions.

Though there are many programs for mentoring today that include all women (and men), sometimes called "accountability partners," there is also a higher awareness of the need for mentoring in specific situations: a young woman who is in crisis needing a mentor; a woman in a difficult marriage; a family struggling with a prodigal child. These are hard situations and some women may be afraid of their own ability to deal with such situations. The need for mentors is something God saw centuries ago and it remains a real need in our communities today.

I have been given many objections (excuses), especially by older women who have been approached about mentoring a   younger woman.

- *I don't have time.*
- *I don't know the Bible well enough.*
- *I have done my teaching, it's someone else's turn.*
- *My marriage wasn't so good, what would I have to tell someone else?*
- *I am too busy.*

Some of these are based on selfishness, some on fear. Not one is based on the Word of God. I have heard all of these excuses, and more. Even "I hate to cook." (I still haven't understood how this would be an obstacle to mentoring.) This kind of thinking prevents us from investing in the life of another.

The Bible does excuse some women from mentoring. If we look at Titus 2:3-5 again, it says,

Older women likewise are to be reverent in behavior, not slanderers or slaves to much wine. They are to teach what is good, and so train the young women to love their husbands and children, to be

self-controlled, pure, working at home, kind, and submissive to their own husbands, that the Word of God may not be reviled.

Clearly, according to these verses, if a woman is irreverent, a slanderer, a drunk, or any combination of the three, she should not mentor younger women. Perhaps as you read that sentence you saw something of yourself, maybe a hidden sin in your own life. If so, will you seek a friend or mentor who can help strengthen you as you seek God's help to overcome the sin and serve Him?

Beyond this, we have little excuse not to step up and teach others. We will see that this does not always need to be done formally. Adopting a lifestyle of "teaching" is instructed in the Word of God for the benefit of the children of God. This may be intentionally teaching someone or it may be setting an example of a holy life by the way we live. We will apply this to those in our homes, churches, and who God places in our lives any time He will.

Who Benefits?

It is generally understood that friendly relationships are good for us. We benefit from having someone who cares about us and whom we also care about. Is that also true for a mentoring or discipling relationship?

The commands the Bible gives us do not use the word "mentor" though they do imply a mentoring relationship, if we define mentoring as being "a teacher or a coach." In the passages we already reviewed - Deuteronomy 6:6-9, Titus 2:3-5, and Matthew 28:19-20 - they all point to very different relationships and areas of service for God's people. Yet, they all have one thing in common: the instruction to teach. They all speak to us about how we are to pass biblical truths to the next generation.

You see, mentoring is all about the next generation. As women called by God, we have a responsibility to teach and train the next generation of women to love God, His Word, their husbands, their children and their friends, and to live lives passing this love to even the next generation.

Consider the following verses.

- *And God said, This is the sign of the covenant that I make between me and you and every living creature that is with you for all future generations.* Genesis 9.12

- *And I will establish my covenant between me and you and your offspring after you throughout their generations for an everlasting covenant, to be God to you and to your offspring after you.* Genesis 17.7

- *God also said to Moses, "Say this to the people of Israel, 'The LORD, the God of your fathers, the God of Abraham, the God of Isaac, and the God of Jacob, has sent me to you.' This is my name forever, and thus I am to be remembered throughout all generations."* Exodus 3.15

- *You are to speak to the people of Israel and say, "Above all you shall keep my Sabbaths, for this is a sign between me and you throughout your generations, that you may know that I, the LORD, sanctify you."* Exodus 31.13

- *Know therefore that the LORD your God is God, the faithful God who keeps covenant and steadfast love with those who love him and keep his commandments, to a thousand generations.* Deuteronomy 7.9

To sum up the idea of mentoring with God's Word alone:

When we faithfully pass on knowledge of the covenant of God (Genesis 9:12, 17:7), the love of Jesus Christ, and service to the One True, Living God, it is to the benefit of not just the one we mentor, but to the next generation, and to "all future generations" (Genesis 9:12).

That is a lot of benefit for a little bit of effort. Any friendship that may develop from the mentoring relationship is an added bonus.

And these words that I command you today shall be on your heart. You shall teach them diligently to your children, and shall talk of them when you sit in your house, and when you walk by the way, and when you lie down, and when you rise. Deuteronomy 6:6-7

Start At Home

When my children were little and I had not yet become a Christian, I battled with the decision about whether it was better to stay home and raise my children or go to work in the world and let someone else have my kids eight hours a day. I made a compromise on the issue and worked a few hours a week but was home more than I was away. At the time I was sure I had the best of both worlds.

When I became a Christian I experienced some guilt about those years, especially when I learned about the Proverbs 31 wife. She is an excellent wife who works very hard (inside and outside of her home), but she is also a woman whose obvious priority is her God and her family. Home takes precedence over the things of the world. This made her husband trust her. He was blessed by her work and her children loved her. Proverbs 31:26-27 tell us something of her lifestyle,

She opens her mouth with wisdom, and the teaching of kindness is on her tongue. She looks well to the ways of her household and does not eat the bread of idleness.

These words come after sixteen verses describing how she contributes to the needs of her household, how she cares for the poor, and her secure attitude about the future. All of these attributes cause her children to call her "blessed" and her husband to praise her!

She is living out the Deuteronomy 6:7 call to teach her family, *when you sit in your house, and when you walk by the way, and when you lie down, and when you rise.* She teaches them by example how she wants them to live. Proverbs 31:26 tells us the words coming from her mouth teach wisdom and kindness. According to scripture, wisdom begins with the fear of God (Proverbs 9.10) and kindness is a fruit of the Spirit (Galatians 5.22).

As it was for the Proverbs 31 woman, the obvious place to start teaching at home is with the Word of God. It is where wisdom comes from. We cannot teach what we do not know. If we are to teach our children the Word of God from what is stored in our hearts then, obviously, it has to be stored in our hearts. The very storing of the Word, helps us to stay away from sin.

I have stored up your Word in my heart,
that I might not sin against you. Psalm 119:11

Storing it in our heart requires a consistent time in the Word of God that goes beyond the Sunday sermon. Sunday sermons are good and very useful for spiritual growth when they are based on Scriptures. But, if we are going to hide His Word in our heart then we must spend more time with the Lord, learning who He is and what His Word says.

Intentional With The Lord

Spending time with the Lord has to be intentional. In order to have a personal quiet time with the Lord every day we have to plan for it. Reading and studying God's Word requires discipline. Many people use study guides so they will be forced to think about the Word, not just to read it. I confess I am one of them. When I read the Bible without the discipline of looking for answers to questions, my mind wanders. I am reading the Scriptures, but not thinking about the words. Other people use devotionals that have been written so they do a reading a day. You can find them on a specific topic or a daily, randomly-chosen scripture for each day.

Perhaps you feel like your schedule is so full you don't have time for a personal quiet time. You will need to honestly examine your priorities. Ask God to show you if there is something else that could be removed. Are you doing works someone else could or should be doing? What is eating up your time?

A young mother came to me once after I had been teaching about taking time to be in the Word of God every day. She was feeling very guilty as she had become very addicted to computer games. She was wasting hours playing with no eternal value. She had been making excuses about why she could not possibly make time for devotions during her day with two small children. She became convicted to change her pattern of behavior, because she sensed the need to hide the Word of God in her heart. It took precedent over winning a game.

In the world of effortless internet access, it's easy to become addicted to games, social media, or even to become a news or weather junkie. There is a possibility we could all be spending more time than necessary on the computer, phone, iPad, and other electronic devices. Take a close look at your own time. How are you spending it? Minute-by-minute, how do you spend your time?

Some mothers of young children tell me they cannot get away from their children in order to take the time to sit with the Lord. Certainly, our children need to be a priority and if someone is hurt, hungry, or afraid, we need to attend to them. There are, however, ways to take time with the Lord without hurting, and in fact, benefitting our children. Though our children need to be a high priority, they cannot be our highest priority. Our God has reserved that spot for Himself.

Because my children were older when I came to know the Lord, it was easy for me to train them. Often, I spent time with the Lord while they did schoolwork or were otherwise occupied. Other distractions were more of an issue for me. The computer, the phone, the housework, were all temptations I promised myself I could get to after a time of devotion to the Lord. Most days I succeeded. Some days I failed. I had to learn to prioritize. It was an act of discipline to stay in the Word of God when I first became a Christian.

I once studied with a Mom who said her children were taught they were to stay upstairs and relatively quiet while she was doing her devotions. They learned, after a training period, this time with the Lord was a priority for their Mother. She admitted some days during the training her 8-year-old son would stand at the top of the stairs and repeatedly yell down to her, "Mom, are you done yet?" She ignored him and continued her devotions. Now, that takes some patience and determination!

This is not to say missing a day is a big deal. There may be short periods of time when an illness, a sick child or other responsibilities take all of our time and energy. These do not change the fact that knowing, storing in our heart, and applying the Word of God to our lives, needs to be a high priority for the woman of God.

When we have that nagging feeling, that conviction, that daily devotions are something we need to get started (or get back to), be encouraged! That is the Holy Spirit calling us back to the Lord. We all know that the more time we spend with someone the better we get to know them. The Lord wants us to get to know Him so we will want to draw even closer.

Know this: If you really are too busy to spend time with the Lord, *you are too busy*. Someone once taught me "busy" is an acronym for "Bound Under Satan's Yoke." He wins if we fail to learn Scripture well enough to teach our children. And, because our children generally follow our example with their children, he may win over the next generation as well.

Our own time spent with the Lord will set an example. Do your children see and hear more about social websites (like Facebook, Twitter, Instagram) than they do the Word of God? Are there more conversations, and more time spent, in front of television shows than the Word of God? The way we live is a reflection of our priorities and, by example, will set theirs.

If you are not regularly studying God's Word, will you examine your busy schedule and see what can be removed? If we understand Deuteronomy 6:6-7 correctly, all day long we have opportunities to teach the Word of God - *when we sit in the house, when we walk by the way, when we lie down, and when we rise.* Our children will see and hear our faith in the way we live. The words we use in response to God's creation, reactions to the deeds (good and bad) of other people, and the way we spend our time will speak truths about our reliance on Him and His Word. The truth is, when we are with our children we are teaching them by example if not by words. Make no mistake. They are watching.

Pass It On
My family has a tradition of watching the movie "White Christmas" every year in December. Recently I heard my thirty-two year old daughter joking with my husband that she can come up with a song to sing from that movie in almost any situation that arises. Imagine this. If we know a movie this well watching it once a year for thirty years, how well would we know our Bibles if we were in them daily for at least that many years, or even more? When we are in it so much that we know what God has said - even if we can't quote chapter and verse - there is never a situation that arises to which a biblical principle cannot be applied. When we consciously do that with our children, they too, will learn the principles God teaches in His Word.

In addition to personal time with the Lord, Bible studies are great places for mothers to study the Scriptures. A good study will teach the Word of God, offer a place for spiritual growth and can be an encouragement as women fellowship with others trying to raise their children, or be an influence with grandchildren, in the discipline and instruction of the Lord. An intergenerational group is especially a blessing as it provides the wisdom of women from a range of ages and experiences. For those without children in the house, these are places to learn and fellowship with like-minded women. There are opportunities to strengthen and build each other up in the faith (Ephesians 6:4). The greater our bonds with the body of Christ, the more devoted we will be to Him as we practice spurring one another on to love and good works (Hebrews 10:24).

Bible studies will also help equip us to know and understand how to learn the Word of God well enough to teach it.

- We are to meditate on the Word (Joshua 1:8). This means paying attention and thinking about it as we read it.
- We are to store it up in our hearts (Psalm 119:11). In other words, be in it frequently so we know it well enough to remember it when we need it.
- We are to listen to it when we are being taught. Just being present for a sermon or bible study is not enough. We must have our minds engaged with what the speaker is saying so we can learn from him/her (Luke 11:28).
- We are also to allow God's Word to light our paths (Psalm 119:105). Whatever we do should be compared to the scriptures, held up to the light of the Word of God. Is it right, is it kind, is it just, is it godly behavior? If the light the Word of God sheds exposes a sin, then we need to turn from whatever it is we are doing.
- Last, we are to teach it (2 Timothy 4:2). We should take any opportunity we have to speak the truth to someone else.

Every Christian needs to be in a Bible preaching church (Hebrews 10:25). The teaching and the fellowship will enrich our lives as we learn God's Word. We, and our families, will reap the benefits of knowing what He says.

Personal time in the Word of God, a group Bible study, times of worship and fellowship, and reading good books written for the purpose of growing our understanding of God's Word, are all ways we can learn it and how to apply it to our lives. After that, where and how we study the scriptures will be determined by the other circumstances of our lives. That we do it is important. The way we do it is up to the individual.

Once there is a plan in place for learning the Word of God, begin to teach as you go. Some of the best conversations my own family have at the dinner table are around a question coming from a study of the Bible. Many seem to think they cannot teach until they reach the level of biblical scholar. Not true. When you learn something new, share it.

When our daughter was a sophomore in a large, urban high school, she came home with a question which she shared at the dinner table. The kids at her lunch table were using bad language. I don't know how the conversation got started but a boy challenged her when she commented on his choice of vulgar words. He said something to the effect of, "Why do you care, the Bible doesn't say I can't use that word."

We were relatively new Christians, not even owning a concordance. She knew he was wrong, but she did not know how to counter him. She wanted chapter and verse and I could not give it to her. All we had to work with were the small concordance pages at the back of our Bibles.

We looked up "cuss," "curse" (which we learned a lot about that day), "word," "words," and any other related term we could think of. Finally, one of us (I don't remember who anymore) came up with "language" and Colossians 3:8 showed up on our radar. There it was, *remove filthy language from your lips.* We knew very little, but the Lord honored us with success in our daughter's desire to speak up for Him. And, we all learned something from searching the Scriptures.

Meals, eaten as a family, are one of the tools every family has for talking about the Scriptures. Sadly, more and more families are so busy with worldly distractions (sports and social media) they are no longer taking time for the family to sit down together to eat. I strongly urge you to reinstate "dinner time" (if you are not doing so now), and to encourage others to as well. A lot can be learned about what is going on in the mind of a child who is sitting at the table. Many years ago our pediatrician taught us that kids are always moving something.

If you sit them still at the table (or buckle them into a car seat), their mouths will move. As they speak, we can apply God's truths to their ideas and understanding. Opportunity knocks at the dinner table!

Deuteronomy 6 is clear we are not just to teach our children, but to teach them diligently. If we are diligent, we will be attentive to the task constantly, looking continually for opportunities to teach what God's Word says about the current situation. The teaching will be intentional, thoughtful, and we will persevere in it. And, God is faithful to bless those who obey His commands.

You shall teach them diligently to your children, and shall talk of them when you sit in your house, and when you walk by the way, and when you lie down, and when you rise. Deuteronomy 6:7

These words allow no time for relaxing the standard of teaching. Add to that mandate, this one:

You shall bind them as a sign on your hand, and they shall be as frontlets between your eyes. You shall write them on the doorposts of your house and on your gates. Deuteronomy 6:8-9

These are instructions to put reminders in place, to remember what we are supposed to be doing. If God's law is dangling from our hands, and directly in front of our eyes, and even written on our doorposts and gates, how could we forget the charge we have to teach our children? The Word of God would be before us all the time, the same time we are to be teaching them.

Obviously, most of us are not out and about with anything dangling from our hands or right in front of our eyes. If any woman wants to teach her children the Word of God, or be prepared herself to teach them, what would this look like in our day?

How many Bibles do we have laying around our homes? Are we willing to get those words off the pages in practical ways we can use to teach them and be reminded of them? We can be creative about ways to get God's Word before our own eyes and the eyes of our children. Some families memorize from cards they create and go over several times a day. I once worked with a woman who said she had her children read the same verse with each meal, three times a day. They would learn the verses in just a couple of days. Others tack them to a mirror or in the bathroom, over the kitchen sink or on a desk next to the computer to remind themselves not to look at worthless things.

(Psalm 119:37). We can frame them and have them hanging in our homes.

I once heard a Sunday sermon from a guest preacher named Jake Susex who said "If your Christianity is not working at home, do not export it." This is sound advice. If we are not willing or able to teach our own children the Law of God then we should not be concerned with mentoring others. Those at home should be our top priority.

Helpful Resources

As Christians (though it is true for everyone), we cannot underestimate a mother's importance in the lives of her children. Mothers (and fathers) are their children's comforter, provider, protector, law-giver, and teacher -- in short, parents are the representative of God in their children's lives. No other human or agency has the understanding or the best interests in mind for her children. As mentors to our children, we must start at home. It would also be difficult to overemphasize these truths to mothers.

When our daughter was a first grader in public school, she had been in a private pre-school and was academically ahead of others in her class. We felt she had been placed in the wrong classroom, with the wrong teacher, for various reasons. I had two sisters teaching in another district at the time and called one of them to see what she thought. Her words were true and convicting. "Beth, no one cares about her like you do. You are her only advocate." It gave me the encouragement to push for what I thought she needed.

So much is happening in our nation with regard to the Christian faith. It is hard to care diligently for our children, from a spiritual perspective, as we send them into the world. Public schools and other public forums do not respect Christianity and feel fully justified in teaching children anti-Christian principles. More diligence is required as our children are exposed to more of the world. We are their advocates in a world that condones a very different perspective.

There are many excellent books written on Christian parenting by people who did a far better job at it than I did. One of my great regrets in life is that my husband and I did not come to know the Lord until our children were pre-teens. Oh, to have those young years back to rear them in the nurture and admonition of the Lord. As mentors and sisters in Christ, we will be offered opportunities to encourage younger women to pour the Word of God into their children. The children will have a great start to their own lives when they do. This is the kind of help mentors can offer that will, hopefully, have a generational influence.

To be "diligent" in our quest to live and teach the fear of the Lord that leads to wisdom requires Christian parents to consider every influence entering the lives of our children. Parenting books may not deal with some of the overarching issues of outside influences parents have to deal with today. There are many resources offering biblical perspectives on public education, homeschooling, Christian school, and other organizations that our children are being pulled into in today's world. Now, more than ever, it is important to know what our children will be exposed to in any school setting or extra-curricular clubs and activities.

Mothers need to clearly understand the biblical priority of their own children. Teaching young women to start at home, diligently teaching their own children the Word and the ways of God, will have a lasting, generational effect. Children are a blessing and a delight to others when they are raised in the fear and admonition of the Lord. God has entrusted them to us to teach and to train for His glory, so they will teach and train their children when the time comes.

3
Intentionally Intergenerational

Older women likewise are to be reverent in behavior, not slanderers or slaves to much wine. They are to teach what is good, and so train the young women to love their husbands and children, to be self-controlled, pure, working at home, kind, and submissive to their own husbands, that the Word of God may not be reviled. Titus 2:3-5

Mix and Match Generations

In my local church we recently ran a program for wives and mothers led by the older women in the church. We used a six-week "canned" program [1] designed to follow Titus 2:3-5 with lessons on kindness, loving your husband, loving your children, purity, submission, and hospitality. Each of the six weeks involved a dinner in which three younger women sat at a table with two older women. The conversations at the table were loosely structured to coincide with the topic of study for the evening. Unanimously, this was the favorite part of the evening for the younger women. Attendance for the once-per-week, six-week study was fabulous. One woman missed one week for a vacation planned before the class started. Otherwise ten young wives, seven of them mothers to a total of nineteen children, had perfect attendance. (Kudos to their husbands!)

Attendance and feedback confirmed for me that younger women are hungry for intergenerational relationships. Mothers and grandmothers are not always available, and they are not always Christians. Unfortunately, in some churches the structuring of "programs" prohibits such interaction beyond the immediate family.

The Problem

Over time I have heard from women in church after church about limited opportunities for intergenerational interaction. Many times it

---

[1] Betty Huizenga ,"Apples of God, A Six-week Nurturing Program for Women", Colorado: David Cook, 2000

seems the organizers have not anticipated the long-term consequences of separating the generations. The biblical mandate for the older women to teach the younger women is sometimes lost in the creation of "new opportunities."

Some churches are quite deliberate in establishing separate events for the young mothers, the young single women, the middle-aged women, and the older women. This is even true for Bible studies. The younger women have very little interaction with the older women, presenting an impediment to obeying this command. When the members of a congregation are segregated by age (deliberately or inadvertently), a young woman seeking a "trusted advisor" in a mentor has few opportunities to get to know the older women well enough to approach them.

The distance can cause misunderstanding. A woman from another congregation once asked me if I would mentor her. She was a relatively young widow with a teenaged son. She was hitting a rough spot in parenting and looking for someone to speak truth into her life as she knew she was not trusting the Lord in her situation.

For accountability and proximity, I always try to point women back to their own churches to seek a mentor. She objected, saying there was no one she thought could understand her issues. I happened to know a mature woman, also a widow, in her church who I thought would be a great match for her. My suggestion was rejected because the younger woman thought the older woman was "too perfect, she could never understand." She based her understanding on the way the older woman was dressed each week. But I was sure this was not the case.

This older woman had lived through the rebellious teenage years of one of her own children. She has a grandson abusing drugs and worked hard to keep her eyes on the Lord as she struggled with losing her own husband. Younger women in her congregation do not know because they have little opportunity to interact with her. From a distance she apparently looks like she has had it all together all her life and would not understand the struggles of another woman.

One of the realities older women may face is the position we hold in the eyes of the younger women. When there has been little interaction, they may be somewhat intimidated to approach us if   they think we would make a good mentor. We need to find a way to make it known that we are willing and will take the time. It may be engaging the younger women in conversation by observing their countenance: "You look happy today." "You seem tired today." or "Wow, your children were so well behaved during the service this morning. You must work hard at teaching them."

We can also create our own opportunities by inviting younger women for coffee or lunch, or ask them to help you with a project in a church ministry. We may want to let a leader of the church know we are willing so we can be suggested as they engage in conversation with the younger women.

The Challenge

Older women, the charge is ours to get to know the younger women. We must be intentional in our churches to create times to mingle with younger women. We need to deliberately engage them in conversation. We may want to serve alongside them in classrooms, Vacation Bible School, and on various committees so we can take time to get to know them.

When my husband and I first became Christians, we moved from our "secular" church where the Bible was not taught and found a Bible-preaching church. At the time we had teenagers and the first people we got to know were other people with children the same ages as ours. Because of our children, we were thrown into "social" situations where we could talk and get to know other adults (even if it was in a parking lot waiting for the Youth Group bus to get back.)

Later, at the ages of 55 and 56, we changed churches. The "child advantage" was gone. Getting acquainted with others our age was much more difficult. People are set in their "cliques." We were warmly welcomed on Sunday mornings and on committees for service. People were very kind to us anytime we showed up. But there is little time offered to interact with others, even our own age, no less younger women who were given their own separate opportunities to gather and study.

Here is a place we must become intentional. If we want openings to teach and train younger women, we may have to make them. Titus 2:3b says older women are to teach. It is a command.

Interestingly, one of the things Titus 2 tells us to teach is *to work at home*. One of the ways people learn is by seeing an example. Hospitality is more and more a lost art since women work and eat out more than ever before (often on the run from one commitment to another). Women are spending less time "working at home" and less time in each other's homes than the women of previous generations. Though your home may not be spotless, would a show of hospitality, an invitation, demonstrate a welcoming or a well-organized home to someone who does not have that example? Would it open up a conversation about how to be busy at home? Would it demonstrate that hospitality need not be formal and spotless?

Why not invite a younger couple over for dinner or several young women to come for tea? There is much to learn from women sitting around a table chatting about life. People around a table tend to talk, especially if there is good food giving them reason to stay.

Two of the churches we have attended sponsored "Growth Groups" or "Small Groups." In both churches we witnessed "older" couples not wanting the hassle of small children attending their groups. Certainly, times to meet, the food served, and dynamics of the group change when children have to be considered. But we must pause and consider: Can this be a biblical attitude? Should we be encouraging these groups to be intergenerational? Making accommodations for the "mix" could certainly steer the teaching and training in an intergenerational direction as a natural part of the group's study and fellowship. Certainly, an older and a younger woman would have enough interaction during those time to know if they would be a good "one-on-one" pair, or even good friends. (This would also be true for the older and younger men who have time to fellowship that they may not otherwise have.)

Sunday mornings are another opportune time to interact intergenerationally. They are often missed because we are in a hurry, or we are too afraid to approach someone we do not know well. The Lord tells us not to neglect meeting together (Hebrews 10:24-25). In Acts 2 we learn of the first church, *And they devoted themselves to the apostles' teaching and the fellowship, to the breaking of bread and the prayers. (Acts 2:42)*

Intentional Influence

Many churches are good at the teaching and the praying but fall short in fellowship as congregants rush out of the building to get to the next event. Is there really something so important happening right after church that we cannot afford to take our time leaving the building? This is a time we can use as an opportunity to engage another woman in conversation.

Today's culture of divorce, cohabitation, "doing our own thing," and abuse leads to much pain, fear, and guilt. Much of this is happening in the church as well as in the world. There are many women living in shame or guilt because of an abortion or physical or sexual abuse in their history. They fear speaking the truth, afraid of judgment rather than grace. If we were to approach other women on Sunday mornings just as a way of getting to know them, would we later be the one that could help or point them to those who can help? When we leave church quickly every week, we leave the impression we are not interested in others.

Every relationship starts somewhere. A consistent greeting and kind words may lead someone to trust us enough to start a conversation about deeper things. It might start with a few words in the pew week after week and progress to a cup of coffee in your home or hers before trust has been established. If a woman needs help, the way we deliver our words and kindnesses could lead to a deeper level over time. It seems that some women read us for sincerity and willingness to bear the other's burdens before engaging with us on a more personal level.

Another scenario may be one of a young wife and mother overwhelmed by the amount of effort, emotion, and stamina required to keep up with a home, a husband, a few children, and possibly, work outside of the home. Does she need to hear from someone about ways to organize the chaos so she still has energy at the end of the day (or to start the day)? Sometimes talking to someone who has already been through it, who kept her eyes on the Lord, is the instruction she needs to hear.

Many older women are no longer held down or consumed with what needs to be done in their own homes. Some of us have grown children, less laundry, less mess, and more time. The Bible says we should share that time with young women who want to love their husbands and children, to serve the Lord, and grow in faith and understanding of the One True God.

Willing Servant

Are we willing? Are our Women's Ministries preparing women to love one another? Serve one another? Encourage one another? Admonish one another? Even to befriend one another for good Christian fellowship? Do our pastors know we would be willing to come alongside a younger woman who wants to grow in the Lord? Would we be willing to approach her ourselves to offer to mentor or disciple her?

If you are an older woman and you are resisting these suggestions, will you pray you would be willing to do what God commands with regard to teaching younger women? No one can do everything or mentor everyone, but each of us can examine our own gifts and talents and look for how we can be used to serve and encourage a younger woman. Will you pray for the Lord to show who He has for you to come alongside of in your own congregation or neighborhood? Let your Pastor know you are willing; it will take a load off him to have a willing helper he can call on when the need arises.

The safest and most secure place a Christian can be is in the center of the will of God. He has called us to this ministry of mentoring. In future chapters we will talk about some of the different ways God has gifted women to serve one another as mentors. He has given us many options regarding the way we can use our various gifts to minister to younger women.

What fears are keeping you from obedience to this command to teach younger women?

4
Disciple Makers

Go therefore and make disciples of all nations, baptizing them in the name of the Father and of the Son and of the Holy Spirit, teaching them to observe all that I have commanded you. And behold, I am with you always, to the end of the age. Matthew 28:19-20

I love to teach ladies' bible studies. After stepping away from Bible Study Fellowship (BSF) I was teaching at my local church. After the first year I ran into a lady who had been in BSF. She and some other women had been doing a study but the woman who had been leading them was not going to do one the next year. She asked me if I would teach. I was sure God was giving me the desire of my heart.

As I had been in conversations with other women over the years, I was growing concerned about how little the women surrounding me, not necessarily those in the study, but Christian women in general, knew of the Old Testament. The Bible study offered me an opportunity to encourage Old Testament study.

We started studying 1 Samuel, and the ladies really seemed to enjoy it. The following semester we studied 2 Samuel, and amazingly, the study was growing. One woman invited and brought a friend who was in her sixties. She had never opened a Bible. At the end of the study, she told us she had come to know the Lord! I was very excited God would choose to use this Bible study of 2 Samuel to bring this lady to saving faith. She has now studied 1 and 2 Kings with us as well.

I saw spiritual growth but was concerned about her study being only from the Old Testament books, fearing there may be parts of the gospel she did not fully understand. As we came near the end of our study in May one year, I asked her if she would like to be "discipled." She was very happy for the offer. She and I met for several weeks.

This woman is now over seventy years old. She has been divorced for many years, her grandchildren are in their teens. Her greatest needs were not so much the practical working out of the wife and family life of Titus 2 as they were growing as a disciple of Jesus Christ. What a gift God gave me as we met together around His Word.

We studied from a book called "Growing in Christ."[2] I like to call it "Christianity 101" because it is a study guide divided into thirteen lessons of the basics of Christianity. She did the study before I arrived at her home each week. She and I went over the questions one by one. Some of them only ask for what a verse says, others prompt a little more conversation, so it stayed interesting for both of us. She had taken in every verse the book directed her to and soaked up the truth of what it taught. I was able to see her faith growing from week to week. The book covered topics on the: Assurance of Salvation, Forgiveness, Answered Prayer, Victory, Guidance. Then it moved on to lessons on Christian living which included: Putting Christ First, His Strength, His Word, Love, Giving, The Church, Good Works, and it ended with Witnessing.

I do not expect this little study guide, and a few meetings with me, to suddenly create a mature disciple of Jesus Christ or to teach all there is to know about what the Bible says on these subjects. The book keeps the topics at an introductory level, leaving a hungry new Christian wanting more. Good conversations regarding each topic are one reason to keep studying, repeatedly taking me back to this resource.

There was a time when many churches would assign a new Christian a mentor, along the lines of what I just described. Over the years, for reasons I do not completely understand, the tide has changed. If someone has a real problem in her marriage or there are some socio-economic concerns, she may be asked if she would like someone to disciple or mentor her. One church I know has replaced this type of assigned mentor for assignment to a small group within the church. Small groups are also effective. They, too, offer spiritual growth to a new believer as they meet and discuss the Bible.

---

[2] NavPress, "Growing in Christ", Colorado: The Navigators

"Make Disciples"

Jesus said, "Go and make disciples." I clearly remember the first time someone pointed out to me that Jesus did not say, "Go and make converts" but had used the word "disciple." A profession of faith does not impress Him as much as living a life of faith.

Sadly, as there is increasing emphasis on numbers in the pews rather than changes of the heart, we will fall farther and farther away from having churches filled with disciples. A person who responds to an altar call or walks an aisle to pray the "sinner's prayer" is not necessarily born again. Jesus' disciples learned from Him, they followed Him, and they imitated Him. This is what we want for every convert, including ourselves; that they would learn from, follow, and imitate Jesus Christ. A conversion should produce a change. A disciple is one who, having received the Holy Spirit through faith, follows the ways and words of Jesus.

The Scriptures speak of different responses to God's Word:

And he told them many things in parables, saying: "A sower went out to sow. And as he sowed, some seeds fell along the path, and the birds came and devoured them. Other seeds fell on rocky ground, where they did not have much soil, and immediately they sprang up, since they had no depth of soil, but when the sun rose they were scorched. And since they had no root, they withered away. Other seeds fell among thorns, and the thorns grew up and choked them. Other seeds fell on good soil and produced grain, some a hundredfold, some sixty, some thirty. He who has ears, let him hear." Matthew 13:3-9

Jesus clearly tells us in these verses not everyone who hears the Word of God, even if they respond to it initially, will be able to produce fruit for the Lord. Later in the chapter He explains it.

Hear then the parable of the sower. When anyone hears the word of the kingdom and does not understand it, the evil one comes and snatches away what has been sown in his heart. This is what was sown along the path. As for what was sown on rocky ground, this is the one who hears the word and immediately receives it with joy, yet he has no root in himself, but endures for a while, and when tribulation or persecution arises on account of the word, immediately he falls away. As for what was sown among thorns, this is the one who hears the word, but the cares of the world and the deceitfulness of riches   choke the word, and it proves unfruitful. As for what was sown on good soil, this is the one who hears the word and understands it. He indeed bears fruit and yields, in one case a hundredfold, in another sixty, and in another thirty. Matthew 13:18-23

Many times people hear the good news of Jesus Christ but, just as He taught, the things of the world come along and take them away. The person who enters into a relationship with a mature Christian for discipleship may either see the sinfulness of her ways and come to Christ sooner than if left on her own, or from a deeper study into God's Word, will see she is not a disciple and leave the church. God is sovereign over the salvation of everyone. If she leaves, He is the One who can draw her back, not us. The mentor need not suffer any guilt because a person rejects the Lord. When God calls, she will return.

A woman who comes to know the Lord, whether from a background of a peaceful, quiet life or one of turmoil and strife, will be better prepared for the Christian life if she has fellowship with other believers. This lesson can be demonstrated in a mentoring or friendly relationship.

My first formal mentoring relationship was to teach a new believer how to follow the Lord Jesus Christ with all her heart, all her soul, all her strength, and all her mind. She had just found out that her husband had committed adultery with someone in his workplace. She had come to the church, which she chose because it was in her neighborhood, to seek some divine help in facing the challenges before her. In a conversation with the associate pastor, she gave her life to Christ. He then came to me and asked if I would disciple her with the "*Growing in Christ*" book (NavPress, previously described).

This is one of the greatest privileges I have ever had. She was hungry for the Word of God, and this study guide took us through basic truths of the faith. As we worked our way through each chapter, the book had us look at the Scriptures teaching the truth to a 34 year old woman who was seeing some of it for the first time in her life. Interestingly, this time the verses led to conversations about her own security being in Christ rather than her husband and the forgiveness she needed to extend to continue in her marriage. God's Word addresses every situation! The seeds planted in her had fallen on good soil.

I can remember questions like, "What is righteousness?" "Am I allowed to listen to Bon Jovi?" "God may forgive my husband but how do I?"

Her faith was growing stronger as God got her through each difficult day until she could see healing in herself and in her marriage. Today she and her husband have added a daughter to their family and her husband was baptized in the same church in 2011. God is good.

For most women becoming a disciple of Christ is not a process stopping at the end of one thirteen-week study. There needs to be an ongoing relationship where she can ask the questions she is afraid will sound "stupid" in a more public setting There are many studies written for women, and many topics covered. Time is required to look through them, maybe even doing the study ourselves before we put it before the one we mentor. Do some research as not everything called a "Bible study" accurately interprets the Scriptures.

Becoming a disciple of Christ is a lifelong process as He sanctifies us through his Word. Maturity will come more quickly for the one who is willing to stay in the study of the Scriptures. It may take months to become a habit they are abiding in. If we want to see long term commitment to Christ, it will take an on-going commitment to His Word. We may feel the call to continue to meet together with them through more than one study.

Jesus defines His disciples in John 8:31-32: *Jesus said to the Jews who had believed in him, "If you abide in my word, you are truly my disciples, and you will know the truth, and the truth will set you free."*

As we attempt to encourage another woman to abide in God's Word, as we love her, and serve her, perhaps even admonish her, we set the example of what it means to be a disciple. The Scriptures remind us to set an example because it is one way people learn.

- *Now these things happened to them as an example, but they were written down for our instruction, on whom the end of the ages has come.* 1 Corinthians 10:11
- *Brothers, join in imitating me, and keep your eyes on those who walk according to the example you have in us.* Philippians 3:17

- *It was not because we do not have that right, but to give you in ourselves an example to imitate. 2 Thessalonians 3:9*

All three of these verses speak of following examples set for us regarding faith in Jesus Christ. Setting the example of a follower, a disciple of Jesus Christ is a high calling. It is a call to commitment, a call to stand firm, and a call coming with a cost, as well as the rewards of joy and peace.

We will sacrifice time and perhaps some resources to have the privilege of watching God work in another woman's life. What a privilege He offers us as we watch Him grow them into examples for others!

5
Whose Work is It?

Cast your burden on the LORD, and he will sustain you; he will never permit the righteous to be moved. Psalm 55:22

As I look back on the women I have mentored, it is interesting to see where they are now. Some are following the Lord wholeheartedly, some half-heartedly, and a couple have little or no fruit that can be seen in their lives. My only contact with some of them is through social media.

As mentors it is important to know and understand our biblical doctrines. If we go into a mentoring relationship with some idealized view of who we are and what we are capable of doing for another person, we will leave it very disappointed and unfulfilled, as will the women we mentor.

Many women want to be mentored because there is some difficult situation in their lives needing to be corrected. Sometimes, they are looking for someone who can "fix it" for them. The Scriptures are clear, the role of the mentor is to teach and train, to set an example, but not to fix problems. The truth is that only the Lord has the power to change her situation. I am grateful for Paul's words in 1 Corinthians 3:7: *So neither he who plants nor he who waters is anything, but only God who gives the growth.*

Starting off with the right (biblical) understanding of who God is and who we are is a great first step in helping to teach or train another woman. God is the source of all power in any woman's life. Through His Word, the Holy Spirit, and her faith in Jesus Christ, she can overcome any set of worldly circumstances. The power lies in God's love, mercy, and compassion for His people, not our wits, Bible knowledge, or sacrifice of time.

Many of the Psalms teach us where our help comes from. In Psalm 103:1-6, David is praising God for all His benefits. He recognizes God as the One who has repeatedly come to his rescue. Whether the struggles were physical or spiritual, God was the One who came to Him in his time of need. Look at the list he gives us in these verses:

Bless the LORD, O my soul, and all that is within me, bless his holy name! Bless the LORD, O my soul, and forget not all his benefits, who forgives all your iniquity, who heals all your diseases, who redeems your life from the pit, who crowns you with steadfast love and mercy, who satisfies you with good so that your youth is renewed like the eagle's. The LORD works righteousness and justice for all who are oppressed. Psalm 103:1-6

Take note, it is God who forgives our sin. It is He who heals our diseases (either here or by taking us to glory). He is the One who can redeem our lives from the pit. While God's goodness and faithfulness are all His own, a woman in a pit in life may need someone to come along side of her and encourage her to seek His assistance. We must acknowledge her pain or grief might leave her with a lack of emotional resources to seek Him. He is the One who loves perfectly and shows mercy. Only He can satisfy us with good. It is through Him that we are renewed in spirit and He empowers us to face life when it gets difficult.

As we mentor, we may run into a woman who is oppressed. There are marriages where women are living with verbal, physical, financial, or sexual abuse (some men are as well). There may be work situations in which a female employee feels oppressed. Especially if the situation is one where she needs the money, but feels like she is being expected by her employers to do unethical or illegal work. She is a Christian, she doesn't't want to sue. Perhaps, no one is listening to her concerns. She needs to reason out what she can do, perhaps just get support and encouragement to look for a new job. The Lord will work her righteousness and justice. She may need someone to help her navigate the waters to safety. A mentor who searches the Scriptures with her will help her discern how to direct her steps according to God's Word.

With prayer and Bible study we are able to help. We can offer her God's Word relating to her heart issues, helping her correct her life issues. God is able, we are not. As mentors our hope, our faith, and our strength come from Him.

When we believe we are capable of helping without Him, we lose any beneficial thing we might offer.

Before I scare you out of ever mentoring, please let me point out this does not require that you become a biblical scholar. The Bible (or any one book) does not have to be memorized. What is required is a heart-desire to do things God's way and to point the women we mentor to God's Word for instruction. This may require some study, a few reference books, or knowledge of how to use a concordance or on-line websites, helping to direct us to the right Scripture.[3]

Spiritual Growth

Spiritual growth or sanctification is very important in the Christian life. One of the fruits of salvation that is exciting to see is a hunger for the Word of God. Obedience to God's commands is part of the fruit of salvation. Many people today who come to know the Lord later in life have had little to no Bible knowledge. They need to learn God's Word. The only person whose spiritual growth we are responsible for is our own. If we take on the burden of responsibility for the spiritual growth of the women we mentor, we will burn out quickly. They are accountable before God for the time and study they put into growing their faith. Remember, we are but an instrument God can use to point others in His direction.

When God is at work, we will see hunger for the His Word in the women we mentor. We do not put spiritual hunger there, nor can we take credit for it. It is God's work and it is a joy to see it in action! This truth is a blessing! 2 Peter 1:10 says, *Therefore, brothers, be all the more diligent to make your calling and election sure, for if you practice these qualities you will never fall.*

We are to be diligent in our own calling and election. If the women we mentor are doing, or not doing, what they need to do to grow in faith and knowledge of the Lord, we are not responsible. We can lead the horse to water, but we cannot make her drink. Our responsibility is

---

[3] I often use biblegateway.com, blueletterbible.com, or E-Sword. If I want to know what the Bible says about something I go to these resources and do a keyword search. Over the years I have learned the words the Bible uses in the ESV. Sometimes I will know a verse from having memorized it in Sunday School as a child (though there are not many of those). With either of these tools I can change versions to look for the verse I need, as a child most of what I learned came from the King James version. Sometimes I have to "play with it" for a while before I find the verse I am looking for but eventually, the Lord will lead me to what I need.

to make sure the water we lead them to is the true Living Water of Jesus Christ. When she does drink we want it to be good for her.

Pray, Pray, Pray
The bottom line here is to trust God and teach those we mentor to trust Him. Every mentoring relationship will necessitate some time in prayer.

- Pray you will be sensitive to the leading of the Holy Spirit in what resources and Bible passages to use.
- Pray for a sincere love and concern for the one you mentor.
- Pray for a warm friendship and open fellowship to come from the relationship.
- Pray for her spiritual growth.
- Pray for her handling of the difficult situations in her life that are causing her concern.
- Get to know how to pray for her family and marriage.
- Be her biggest fan, her most enthusiastic encourager, and her best model of a servant of God.

No sweat, right?

Please notice, some of these prayers are for ourselves. We need to keep our own responsibilities and affections before the Lord in prayer so we are able to keep our commitment to the relationship. This is an intentional way to help us stay obedient to the Word of God and attentive to the needs of the women we mentor.

Remember, *I can do all things through Christ who strengthens me. Philippians 4:13.*

6
Beginning The Relationship

Therefore encourage one another and build one another up, just as you are doing. 1 Thessalonians 5:11

Several years ago a business acquaintance of my husband's came to the U.S. from Uruguay to attend a few days of meetings. He brought his wife along, and one night we went out to dinner together. His English was good, and we talked for a while about the differences in the American and Uruguayan cultures. In his country he is a wealthy and well-known man. During our conversation he talked about the need to "manage his friendships." It was a new concept to me. It sounded very controlling. As the conversation proceeded, I understood that we were having a Spanish-to-English problem. He intended to convey that he pays close attention to his friendships. He tries not to let anger or hurt feelings go unnoticed or unattended.

Since I have been mentoring other women, I have noticed that some women do "manage" the relationship so we remain close. This is a good thing. When we mentor another woman, we are entering into an intentional relationship, a friendship. Relationships can be complicated but they can also be rewarding. Whether a woman is seeking help through an emotionally difficult time, or she wants to grow spiritually, a mentor is wise to pay attention as the relationship progresses.

Managing Me First

Most women who are in a position to mentor do not lack friends. They also may have a husband and parents, full time work, children who need to go places or grandchildren to love and influence. These are a lot of relationships and it may call for management! Not management of the people, but management of our own time and emotional resources, as well as spiritual strength.

I highly recommend every mentoring relationship start with a meeting, an interview, to decide if the people, the circumstances, and the commitment are compatible. It is important to know what a mentee is expecting. I have had a couple of examples that helped lead me to this conclusion.

Both situations required more than a weekly, one hour meeting. These women were in trouble in their marriages with verbally abusive husbands. Both were afraid to continue to fight the battle alone. Of course, going in, there is no way to determine how much time and energy it will take. Bigger problems may (but not always) require bigger amounts of time. Though I was aware the first lady had marital problems as I went into it, I had no idea how little I knew about an emotionally abusive marriage. There was more time involved because I had to do my own study just to try to understand the emotional abuse she was facing.[4]

In the first "interview" it is important to find out what the woman has in mind when asking for a mentor (or accepting the suggestion from a pastor or someone else). Without asking directly, which might prompt her what to say, we need to determine if she is looking for biblical change and spiritual growth, or if she is looking for someone to take care of her problems.

Our culture believes it is fine to sit and "vent" to someone else. This is unfortunate as I cannot find permission to vent anywhere in the Scriptures. In fact, Proverbs 29:11 says, *A fool gives full vent to his spirit, but a wise man quietly holds it back.* In the Bible when someone is "pouring out their complaint," it is to the Lord (Psalm 55:2, 64:1,102:1). For marital problems, often a woman needs to tell the mentor what is happening, but not just to complain. If she is unwilling to accept biblical counsel about the complaint, then she may not be ready to seek real help. This woman's mentoring may start with the biblical perspective of her complaints. Her attitudes and words may need to be compared to the Scriptures. A mentor might be most helpful by teaching her a biblical understanding of her situation.

There are times when I have met with a woman and realized in this first meeting that her issues were greater than my knowledge or

---

[4] A great resource should you ever need it is "The Emotionally Destructive Relationship" by Leslie Vernick. She even includes a chapter for the person who comes alongside of the abused to help. More recently she has written, "*The Emotionally Destructive Marriage.*"

experience could handle. Though I willingly continued to meet with her and study the scriptures, I also recommended a Christian or biblical counselor who I thought was more experienced and capable. Many churches today have a pastoral counselor on staff. Not every woman is ready to admit the depth of the problems in her marriage. It may take time to convince her she needs more than we can offer.

When I started to meet with the second woman, Diane, she had a favorite saying about her husband: "You can't fix stupid." A funny sound-bite that often gets a laugh, but a comment that leaves little hope for her marriage and does not honor her husband or his Creator. She recognized it once we talked about it but she had been using it for some time. (More on Diane in chapter 13.) These can be difficult conversations but they are necessary for God to bless the relationship. Leaving a woman in her sin will not do her, or us, any good and, quite frankly, sabotages any effort for reconciliation.

At first, many women are hopeful a mentor will be able, not just to advise, but to make the changes for them. This is something that could be addressed gently in an interview because, obviously, it cannot work that way. The work, the study, facing the hard things, is for them to do with the help of the Holy Spirit. I always like to think of myself as the one who will hold their arms up in the battle, as Aaron and Hur had done for Moses in Exodus 17. While they held up Moses' hands, Israel would prevail in battle but if they dropped his hands, Amalek would prevail. Aaron and Hur moved in alongside Moses to hold his hands up for the good of all Israel.

Some of the women who come looking for a mentor are facing a real battle. When life brings a battle, who would not want to have someone hold their hands up so they will prevail? A whole family and generations to come stand to benefit, not just the woman sitting in front of us.

We need to be realistic about our own limitations. Not every woman has the personality (or time and energy) to stand with another woman while she goes through hard times. It may be her own schedule or a family situation that is already demanding. Receiving a phone call from a distressed woman might be upsetting to her husband or be disturbing to the family routine. Perhaps the thought of having to go with a woman to speak to church leadership is too intimidating. A woman seeking a mentor will be better off to hear right away you are not suited to the situation rather than investing a lot of time and emotional energy only to find out later she or her issues are too much for you.

Lisa Whelchel wrote a book called *"Friendship for Grown-Ups."*[5] She describes her own journey from having an impenetrable wall around herself to opening up to warm and friendly relationships. When she first started speaking for "Women of Faith," she describes a time when she was at a conference and looking for someone to come alongside her in a real friendship. She wanted someone who could "be there," a lot. Her emotions were raw in the pain of a broken relationship she longed to replace. During one of the talks, a speaker was referring to his mother's best friend, Emmitt, who had helped his mother get through a difficult time in her life.

Lisa was sitting next to Anita Renfro who saw the pain on Lisa's face and leaned over, put her arm around her, and asked quietly, "Do you have an Emmitt?" Lisa cried (she described it as "bawled") and answered, "No, and I really need one." Anita's immediate response was "Well, I would make a sucky Emmitt...but I will pray that God will send you an Emmitt."

What grace! If you know you can't go the distance in a mentoring relationship, don't get into it. Anita Renfro did Lisa Whelchel a huge favor by not promising more than she was capable of providing. The pain of abandonment when you finally think there is someone who will help is devastating. Be honest up front.

Establish Your Guidelines

This first meeting is also a good time to establish some guidelines regarding the time you have to offer. Many women will take the time you have to meet and rarely want or require more. A woman in crisis, however, may need significant amounts of time. Set limits. If your family meal times or your Saturday "date nights" are reserved, let her know those are times you would probably not answer the phone.

---

[5] Whelchel, Lisa, *"Friendship for Grown-Ups,"* Nashville, TN: Thomas Nelson, 2010

Initially, these details may not seem important, or you may later realize you never needed them, but, if the woman who is approaching you to mentor her is in crisis, you may be glad to have them in place.

The good news is most women are not in crisis. They are truly looking to grow in faith and knowledge of the Lord, perhaps looking for how they can serve Him and learn what their gifts are. Many have minor problems adjusting to marriage or children, longing for more of a relationship with their husbands, or a deeper understanding of who God is. All these things are clearly addressed in the scriptures.

There are many methods we can employ to mentor these women. In the next chapters we will talk about three methods:

Chapter 7. Short, Sweet, and Fairly Formal

Chapter 8. Divine Appointments

Chapter 9. A Living Example

Section 2: The Method

7
Short, Sweet, And Fairly Formal

Already the one who reaps is receiving wages and gathering fruit for eternal life, so that sower and reaper may rejoice together. John 4:36

Betsy was a woman I had known from teaching a Bible study. She asked if I would mentor her over the summer when schedules were lighter. I knew her only by name and face. I offered to have a meeting to discuss it. She described herself as a young Mom who wanted to grow spiritually, do some work on parenting, and learn more about being a helpmate to her husband. We decided to do a study together in the remaining weeks of summer.

At our next meeting I kept things pretty formal, though friendly. It had been my experience when I failed to structure the meetings, the mentoring had the potential to become a gripe session more than a growth session. No growth comes from griping!

I was suggesting different parenting and marriage books we might work through. I could see what Betsy wanted was something way more informal. She wanted to meet weekly and bring the issue of the day to talk about. This sounds great, but the truth is it is like going to a church that preaches only topically. Without exegetical preaching, we can just skip over the really hard stuff and only have our ears tickled. We may be convicted by some truths, but many others go ignored.

When we do a study of the Bible, even if it is a topical study like parenting, we cannot skip over the parts we do not want to change. When the book puts a verse in front of us we deal with it. She heard my reasoning and agreed to do a study.

That summer Betsy and I met but she rarely had her lessons done, we rarely talked about anything significant, and she cancelled almost as often as she came. It seemed obvious that her heart was not desiring growth. I am not sure what she wanted from our meetings. Maybe she was just looking for some time out of the house.

I met another woman, Linda, who was the wife of an acquaintance of my husband. She was a brand new Christian, attending a biblically weak church. She was hungry for the Word of God. When we met and she learned that I was a Bible teacher, she started asking questions. I offered to set up another time to talk with just the two of us and she jumped at the opportunity. We did a twelve-week study on the sovereignty of God. She came every week with her lesson completed, eager to discuss what she had learned. What a joy!

Meet For Meat

Betsy and I never got to the meat she had asked for because we never dug into the hard stuff of parenting and marriage. Linda grew spiritually because of her investment in the time we had together and the time she spent with the Lord doing the study.

Usually, when you dig into God's Word with someone, it gets personal. Shared details draw you closer. Conviction of sin and answered prayers lead you toward a greater intimacy. When you get close enough to see God working in the life of another you will care for each other. A relationship, though it may begin formally, will not stay formal for long.

An initial mentoring meeting often has a formal feel unless you already know the mentee. I allow some time in the beginning of every meeting to talk about life in general, what's happening at home, how's she's feeling, etc. If we have discussed specific problems I ask about them. If there is a crisis, we may skip the study to discuss what is happening in detail. I try to make that the exception, not the rule.

A mentor who shows up when she says she will, completes the study she starts, listens intently to the words (revealing the heart) of the mentee, and responds appropriately, will prove herself trustworthy. This is why many mentoring relationships can turn into friendships.

When you meet with someone over the Scriptures, to look at life through the lens of the Bible, a close relationship can develop. This is not to say it always will. Nevertheless, when God offers an opportunity to help another woman grow, to teach and train her for a period, consider it a privilege, even if only for a few weeks.

Some relationships are short term by surprise. Susan, a beautiful young woman came to me a few years ago and said a friend of my daughter's had recommended me as a mentor. I met with her, and she told me she had been a Christian since she was young but never felt close to God. When she gave me her testimony, she said she had answered an altar call because they were giving away purple Bibles when she was seven years old. She wanted one, so she went forward. Never since then had she made another profession of faith but she had studied her Bible.

We started studying a book called *"The Fight"* by John White. It is a study of the many different facets of Christianity and what God expects from His children in each aspect. I think we only got to about the fifth chapter. Looking back I marvel at God's guidance in the choice of this particular book. This young woman was in a fight for her salvation.

Each of the few weeks Susan and I met, she would tell me there were things she could not talk about. She seemed to think lots of Christians her age (early twenties) were very good Christians and the she was a very bad Christian. I had to reassure her "all are sinners." As our time together progressed, she finally told me why she was feeling this way. She had two major unresolved sins, a theft and an adulterous relationship with a married man.

We talked about how to resolve them with confession, repentance, restitution, and stopping any contact with the married man. To her credit, she went first to her father, and he walked her through the process of the theft. As far as I know, she dealt with the married man on her own.

Susan repented. God was glorified. She moved three weeks later.

These short term relationships are a very good thing. They may seem to end abruptly but God has a plan and a purpose. In this case, I pray it was to help this young woman act biblically regarding her sin.

Another young woman, Karen, was referred to me for mentoring by our Pastor. She was a new Christian who had married a man raised in a Christian home. They had come to our area for work, far from either of their families, and had just had their first child. When we met, she seemed like a newlywed in need of direction as she compared herself to the Christian family she had married into. As we met together and got close, she told me many stories of abuse from a stepfather. I could see she needed much more help than I could give her. I pointed her to professional Christian counselors. We continued to meet for several months until they moved to be closer to family.

I would consider both of these relationships formal, as their life issues made it difficult to talk about much else before they moved away. There was never enough time for me to develop a real personal relationship with either of these women. In a few weeks it is difficult to develop a deep friendship even if you discuss some personal things. Sometimes a woman will tell you her deepest, darkest, secret, and regardless of your reaction, she is ashamed and would rather not be friends.

Substance Over Form

Though I call these "formal" relationships, as I said before, the word is more about the structure of the meeting than what goes on between us. When a woman is looking for spiritual growth, set out a clear plan to achieve the goal. Commit to a particular study guide or book of the Bible, a time, a place, and a duration of the meeting and, as much as it is up to you, keep the commitments. Wisdom and understanding come only from the Word of God. (Psalm 119:169)

Informal conversations can and will happen within a formal structure. A woman in any situation may need to talk about what is happening in her home or work. We want to apply the Bible's teaching to all of life, so this is the perfect opportunity to speak truth into her life about how she is living. Often a study will lead you to those topics covering everyday issues. The mentor has to be willing to allow the Holy Spirit to lead the direction of the conversation. As I have said before, occasionally, you may not get much of the study done.

Areas of weakness need to be addressed (hopefully, even our own). If we strictly make our "formal" mentoring times a "stick to the questions in the book" conversation we will be bored, frustrated, and ineffective. So will the women we mentor. Knowledge and faith are good but God wants us to put knowledge into action. If we teach all about God, Jesus, the Holy Spirit, and the Word of God, but fail to convey they are living and active, then we will not advance the Kingdom of God because we are not teaching how to apply the Word of God to all of life.

James says, *faith without works is dead.* In fact, he says, *You see that faith was active along with his works, and faith was completed by his work (* James 2:22). Faith is active *in* works and it is completed   *by* works. If the one we want to assist to grow in faith does not actively live in faith, then she has an incomplete faith. We may feel like we invested a great deal and see little result. Fear not, it is God who gives the measure of faith to each one He calls. If we are faithful to the work He has called us to, He will hold each woman we mentor responsible for the works He has prepared in advance for her to do. Our work is to keep serving meat.

Defined Endings

Short term formal mentoring relationships can have a defined stopping point, agreed upon in advance. Often this can be determined by the length of the Bible study guide or by setting a number of weeks at your first meeting with a plan to re-evaluate at the end of that time.

Sometimes you may leave a short term relationship feeling like there is so much more for the mentee to learn or she is avoiding dealing with some of the truths of Christianity she needs to know. Rest assured, we have a gracious and merciful God. He is faithful to complete the work He starts in each of His children. Leave the relationship making sure she knows you are available for further study or meetings at some later point.

I planted, Apollos watered, but God gave the growth. 1 Corinthians 3:6

Even when God gives us only a short time to meet with someone we want to use that time well. Though the format may be formal, we want the relationship to be sweet. God may use us to start the work and take her somewhere else to complete it. We may be planting or we may be watering the seeds of faith. He will take her to the next step in her faith according to His plan. You may see it when you meet her again or you may not see it until heaven!

8
Divine Appointments

The counsel of the LORD stands forever, the plans of his heart to all generations. Psalm 33:11

God's Providence

Have you ever been out somewhere and run into someone you haven't seen in a long time and it's like you just saw them yesterday? Or you meet someone for the first time at an event, and there is a connection right away and you end up in a deep discussion, often about a real issue happening in her life (or yours) at that time? These conversations can be especially meaningful when the opportunity is used to point the other person to the Lord.

If a real problem is revealed in these conversations, this may be a one-time mentoring opportunity. As Christians we should consider this a "divine appointment" and thank God for His providence in the meeting.

If the time and place are not conducive to discussing the subject then arrange another time, offering to meet over a cup of coffee to talk about this specific topic so the need does not go un-met. I know there are times I have missed this divine interruption in my life. I dismissed the opportunity thinking I did not have time, and thereby gave up the blessing of helping a sister in Christ.

Catching The Blessing

Other times the blessing is missed because of insecurity or false humility. We hear the problem, we know the biblical response, but we are afraid to offer counsel or advice. Sometimes, I feel this insecurity or fear means I may be unprepared at that moment, but still offer to "meet for coffee, bring my Bible, and talk about it," knowing God can do a lot when His people are willing. We cannot promise we have just the right remedy for the problem but we can confidently offer what God has for them.

Mentoring (as well as a Christian friendship) is sometimes iron sharpening iron. Proverbs 27:17 says, *Iron sharpens iron, and one man* (woman) *sharpens another*. We can do this over a couple of meetings or we can do it in one brief conversation over coffee, in the hallway at work, or in the back of the sanctuary on Sunday morning.

My most memorable informal mentoring was done with a young woman in a large Bible Study I was teaching. She came up to me after a lecture and asked if I had a minute. She knew her Bible. She was married and struggling with whether or not to have children. She did not think she wanted them and her husband did. We spent ten minutes together talking about what the Bible says about children, like Psalm 127:3, *Behold, children are a heritage from the LORD, the fruit of the womb a reward*. Then we talked about submitting to the will of God and not to the things of the world (Romans 12:2). When she went away, I had no idea what she was thinking. All I had to offer was God's Word.

2 Timothy 3:16 says, *All Scripture is breathed out by God and profitable for teaching, for reproof, for correction, and for training in righteousness, that the man of God may be competent, equipped for every good work.*

That sister in the Lord is the proud mother of four children today! I had nothing to do with that, I am sure she consulted other people, but she sought the Word of God and it changed her mind. Truly, if we love each person and speak to each of them using God's principles and His Word, He will change their hearts. What a blessing to watch Him work!

The topic of children was one that I had studied prior to that conversation. It may not always be the case to be knowledgeable about a particular topic. Someone recently asked me a question about Adam and Eve related to the Tree of Life. I had to admit that I have never studied the Tree of Life. I know almost nothing beyond where to find it mentioned in the scriptures. I promised to look it up and get back to them. We have to be willing to admit what we do not know.

In a short-term, informal mentoring relationship the conversations are informal, the first meetings are most often not planned, the power to change comes from God's Word, and the Providence of the meeting is His doing. We just get the privilege of relaying the message of His Word. He may or may not allow us to see the outcome in this life!

So, the next time you "just happen" to run into someone at the Mall, in the back of the sanctuary, as you shop in the grocery store, or in a hallway of some other building, will you remember God's Providence? He is sovereign over every detail of our lives. Will you engage her in a conversation? Perhaps the Lord is presenting an opportunity for ministry.

9
A Living Example

Brothers, join in imitating me, and keep your eyes on those who walk
according to the example you have in us.
Philippians 3:17

People Are Watching

"There's more caught than taught" was a favorite quote of a friend
of mine. She usually raised this admonition as we were studying a
really convicting passage of the Bible like Colossians 3. When the
Apostle Paul makes lists of things like, "anger, rage, malice, slander,
and filthy language" or, from Romans 1, "envy, murder, strife, deceit,
maliciousness, gossips, slanderers, and haters of God." She would
remind us how many of these sins are easily "caught" rather than
deliberately taught.

Robert Murray M'Cheyne was an influential Pastor of the 1800's.
He is known for this quote, "My people's greatest need is for my
personal holiness."

Because this man was a pastor, we understand what he is saying.
Who wants to be in a congregation where the pastor preaches the
Word of God on Sunday, but lives his life as he chooses, without
concern for the Lord or His Word, the rest of the week? Christians
want to follow a Godly leader and they watch closely enough to see
when their leader is not Godly.

People love to people-watch. It may be out of curiosity but often
it's to compare their own behavior with others. In doing so, whether
they realize it or not, they set their standards for living by what others
are doing. When we compare ourselves to others we are allowing them
to set the standard by which we live. The reality is that we are not
going to be judged by their standard.

Romans 8:29 says, *For those whom he foreknew he also*
predestined to be conformed to the image of his Son, in order that he
might be the firstborn among many brothers. The One we are to be
conformed to is Christ Himself. By nature we look to what other
humans are doing. We want to imitate them, and indeed Paul

instructed others to imitate him. We learn from one another, by observation or instruction. As mentors, we must be aware of the fact that others who want to follow the Lord will look to anyone who seems to love the Lord for direction and understanding of how to behave.

The example we set is a responsibility for every growing Christian. As we are being sanctified, growing in knowledge and understanding of the Word of God we will be offered more and more opportunities to minister to others. Our example, even in our response to the call to serve, will be observed, critiqued (rightly or wrongly), and possibly imitated by others.

In his first letter to the Thessalonians the Apostle Paul tells them why he was so glad they imitated him and the Lord – so they would become the example for others.

And you became imitators of us and of the Lord, for you received the word in much affliction, with the joy of the Holy Spirit, so that you became an example to all the believers in Macedonia and in Achaia. 1 Thessalonians 1:6-7

So, even though these believers had learned about Jesus while they were going through affliction, they were setting a good example. I wonder what kind of example I set when I am in affliction. People watch our responses to hardship and difficulty, to the everyday stresses of life, work, ministry, and the tasks of one who is "busy at home."

When my children were about junior high age we spent a week of vacation with our church at a Bible Conference Center in the Poconos (the mountains of Pennsylvania). There were teaching times in the morning and evening and free time all afternoon. One afternoon I was sitting at the pool with a woman who eventually became a good friend. She is the mother of nine children who ranged in age from three to about sixteen. We were having a leisurely conversation while she kept an eye on the little ones.

Over the course of the time we sat there every child visited her at least once, wanting something. Every time, with every child, she would acknowledge they were there, allow me to finish my sentence or finish hers, and then very calmly she would say, "excuse me Beth," turn to the child and quietly says, "Yes, (and their name)?"

Her patience was absolutely incredible. I had two children and way less patience for constant interruptions. She was polite, calm, direct with her responses, and would come back to the conversation every time without missing a beat. I was wowed.

I had talked to her about their large family before this. She and her husband believed this was a call from God for them. They were determined to raise each child in the fear and admonition of the Lord. They did it with patience and clarity of the call. These children were the most important work in her life. It was obvious in the way she lived and worked with them.

I was watching and so were all nine of her children.

I was convicted of my own impatience and lack of biblical understanding of parenting. She and her husband continue to be role models for my husband and me regarding parenting and family values.

As women we have many roles: wife, mother, daughter, sister, ministry leader or partner, co-worker, friend, aunt, the list goes on. In each of these roles people are paying attention to how our faith affects the way we live. In each position there is someone catching something of what it means to live as a Christian, or maybe just as a woman.

My husband and I were invited to a Memorial Day Picnic a few years ago after I had dropped 15 pounds between August and May. When dinner was over the hostess commented on the weight loss and told me she had watched what I had eaten at the picnic. I was shocked!

Who knew? We talked about the diet and she went on it and lost at least as much as I had. (Oh, if I could only say I was still following it!)

This is a minor thing, but it is an example of the fact that people see what we do and they will imitate it. Our goal needs to be to set the right example all the time. None of us will achieve this perfectly, but it is the right goal.

What have our children learned about how a wife should treat her husband or a mother should treat her children from watching you and me? Is what we demonstrate the biblical model?

What lessons are being taught to those who were observing you or me about the way to treat friends or co-workers?

Does your (or my) behavior in church on Sunday demonstrate the way we are to speak to or about our Pastors? Are we loving, serving, and encouraging others in our congregations on Sunday mornings?

Sometimes, the message we get from other believers is that lunch reservations are more important to keep than the ministry we might do for one another as we fellowship after the worship service.

Most importantly, what are others learning from us about living in a relationship with Jesus Christ? About dependency on Him? About security in Him? What are other members of our church families learning about what it means to be a servant of God through Jesus Christ?

Though we may not be aware of it, someone is watching the way we live. Being this living example is a form of mentoring we do without any direct effort or intentionality on our part. Younger women are catching more than you and I are intentionally teaching.

10
Faithful Friends

A friend loves at all times, and a brother is born for adversity.
Proverbs 17:17

Many years ago my left foot was run over by a car. My husband was in Iowa on business, though he was planning to travel home the next day. My children were young so my in-laws showed up at the hospital to take them home for the night. The wife of one of my husband's business associates was a good friend. She worked full time with 2 small children of her own. She learned of the accident through her husband and left work to come sit by my bed knowing my husband would not be there while I awaited surgery. She did not want me to be alone. I do not remember the conversation. I do not remember any gifts of flowers or balloons. But I do remember her presence. She listened when doctors talked. She spoke softly and gently, She stayed for several hours. What a friend.

A mentoring relationship may have friendly aspects but friendships are an area of life that we may need to encourage the women of God to think biblically about before entering. Choosing and interacting with other women is something we teach more by example than we are aware we do.

In Genesis 2:18, when God has finished with the creation of the heavens and the earth, He makes the declaration, *It is not good that man should be alone. I will make him a helper fit for him.* We use this verse when we are talking about marriage and our partnerships between wives and husbands. But the general statement God makes first is that it is not good for man to be alone. We were made for fellowship, for friendships, and for one another.

Think of the Trinitarian nature of God. He is Father, Son, and Holy Spirit in One God, three in One. I don't think we can begin to imagine the fellowship going on between these three persons of the Trinity. But, we can see it is part of the image we bear, to be in close fellowship with others. Understanding we are made in the image of

God will lead us to an understanding of this need for fellowship with other people.

The Bible has a lot to say to Christians about their friendships. One of the most important things we can understand and teach from the Scriptures about this is our need to be careful about choosing our friends. Proverbs 12:26 says, *One who is righteous is a guide to his neighbor, but the way of the wicked leads them astray.*

A friend is a person who is close enough to have an influence on us. This verse warns us a friend can enrich our lives or they can ruin our lives – especially before the Lord. Our closest friends need to be godly friends. They are the ones close enough to us to speak truth into our lives and we into theirs. If we live by different standards than a friend, either there will be conflict or we'll come to agree.

Some time ago, I had a friend, the mother of 5 children, who would always say, "if you take a white gloved hand and put it into a bucket of tar, the tar does not get glovey." She was very careful about the friendships she would encourage for her children.

The world considers the Word of God foolish, but it is what every Christian needs to use as the law of life. Let's look at an example of a close friendship from the Scriptures.

In the Book of 1 Samuel Saul is king over Israel and David is gaining attention and receiving honor from the people. He slayed Goliath. He was a valiant warrior so the women used to sing "Saul had killed his thousands and David his tens of thousands." Saul became insanely jealous and wanted to kill David to remove him as a threat to the throne.

During this time the prophet Samuel, at the instruction of God, had anointed David as the next king of Israel. All of David's brothers knew about it and eventually many others came to know, including King Saul and his son, Jonathan. David had been deemed to be the rightful heir to the throne. Do I need to say that the king was not happy his own son would not succeed him, as was the tradition of the day?

David and Jonathan were friends. Initially Jonathan could not believe his father would want to take the life of his best friend. As evidence became stronger and King Saul became more vocal and active with his threats on David's life, Jonathan understood the threat to his friend. Though Jonathan was the one in line for the throne from a human understanding, he was a man of God willing to forfeit the throne to David, as God had determined.

I am impressed with the many ways Jonathan demonstrated his friendship and love for David. He made covenants with David but also in 1 Samuel 18:4 Jonathan made a sacrifice for David. He gave David his robe, his armor, his sword, and his bow. All of these were signs of his willingness to sacrifice the throne to his friend.

Real and growing friendships will require sacrifice. We often hear if we want to have a good friend we must be a good friend. Are we willing to sacrifice time and energy, maybe even a little cash to invest in our friendships? These sacrifices communicate a friend's importance to us. What do you need to sacrifice for a friend? Do you need to give up your pride to apologize for a wrong? Do you need to offer your time? A phone call? A day of helping?

In 1 Samuel 19:1 Jonathan warns David of coming trouble from Saul, confirming David's fears that Saul was trying to kill him. Jonathan does not sugarcoat the truth or avoid the truth. He gives David a warning. 1 Samuel 19:2 says, *And Jonathan told David, "Saul my father seeks to kill you. Therefore be on your guard in the morning. Stay in a secret place and hide yourself."*

Scripture says that Jonathan spoke well of David to Saul (1 Samuel 19:4). In 1 Samuel 20:4 he told David he would do whatever David needed him to do to help him escape from Saul's evil intentions. Later in the chapter Jonathan keeps the promise by informing David what he learns from Saul.

In our own personal relationships we can follow the example of solid friendship set by Jonathan , He made (and kept) covenants with David. He sacrificed for his friend. He warned him when he saw danger. He spoke well of David before his enemy. But he did one more thing, which may be the most important thing we can do for any Christian friend (or mentee!).

In chapter 23 of 1 Samuel, David is on the run. Saul is hunting for him, seeking to kill him but has been unable to find him. David has a gathering of 400 men around him. The Bible describes them as *everyone who was in distress, and everyone who was in debt, and everyone who was bitter in soul, gathered to him. And he became captain over them* (1 Samuel 22:2). This was not a terribly encouraging army, helpful and protective maybe, but they do not sound at all godly.

In the grace of God, Jonathan *"rose and went to David."* He found him without any trouble. The commentaries say he travelled about 30 miles to get to him. He was travelling either on a horse or by foot. No buses were running at the time! Then, once he got there, 1 Samuel 23:16 says, *he strengthened his hand in God.*

Strengthen your hand in God. This is what a Christian friend does.

When I think of David, I remember his skill with a sling shot at taking out Goliath. I remember his faith when God called him a man after God's own heart. I remember how the women sang of his success in battle. I remember how skillfully he persuaded his band of social misfits to be a strong army for Israel, winning battles against the Philistines even as they ran from Saul.

I think if I had been Jonathan I would have been tempted to say things like, "You have nothing to worry about, David, you are so strong, you're so smart! You can outsmart Saul. You can overpower him! You have youth and brains Saul does not have!" I would want to point out that David is able to go in with plenty of self-confidence, knowing he can outwit his enemy.

This is not Jonathan's ploy. Jonathan travels thirty miles to repeat God's promise to David. 1 Samuel 23:17-18, And he said to him, *Do not fear, for the hand of Saul my father shall not find you. You shall be king over Israel, and I shall be next to you. Saul my father also knows this." And the two of them made a covenant before the LORD. David remained at Horesh, and Jonathan went home.*

Jonathan does not point David to his own capabilities. He points David to God's faithfulness. Essentially Jonathan says, "Here is what God said and God keeps His promises." This is God-confidence, not self-confidence.

Fear can erase our memories. In our fear we forget what God's Word says, we forget He keeps His promises, He will be our *very present help in times of trouble* (Psalm 46:1). One of the things I love to teach women to do when difficult times come is "preach to the heart" what they know to be true about God. Reminding ourselves of the truth of who God is and how steadfast His love, how faithful He is to keep His promises, can bring us through those hard situations. But, what a joy to have a friend remind us!

Jonathan strengthened David in the Lord by doing two things.

First, he showed up. Sometimes just the presence of someone who loves us, has our well-being at heart, and who is removed enough to think clearly, can be a real help and encouragement. Just like my friend who showed up at the hospital, we can strengthen and encourage a friend in her time of need. Sometimes we don't even need words. Just the presence of someone who cares can say more than many words. A reassuring touch can say, "I hear it, too," when we get bad news. Eye contact that says, "I understand what you need," can provide a feeling of understanding that someone "gets me" or has heard me.

The second thing that Jonathan did was speak the truth. He did not create superficial, shallow things to say. He gave David truth.

Often, as friends and even as mentors, wives and parents, we couch the truth in some kind of package we think will be easier to hear and accept than the whole truth. When we give someone just a piece of the truth, they may make up the rest, and what they dream up is usually much worse than the actual truth.

Jonathan just repeated the truth as he knew it.

Our presence, God's Word, and a touch or eye contact can be really encouraging and helpful to a friend in her time of need. Will you show up for your friend who needs to be encouraged by your presence? What truth does she need to hear?

Love is An Action Verb

Bear one another's burdens, and so fulfill the law of Christ. Galatians 6:2

Life can get very busy for a woman. If we are juggling close and extended family, work, ministry, and friends, it can be difficult to keep up with everyone. I know there are times when I talk to my closest friends every week or every few days, and other times it seems weeks go by before I realize I haven't spoken to one of them recently. If they needed me I was absent.

Even when we are in regular contact, it can be difficult to discern what our friends need. Many times it is obvious, like my crushed foot.

My friend knew my husband was away and my family does not live near me. She came when she was sure there was a need. Not every situation arising in a friendship is easy to read or understand.

We need to evaluate each situation. Does it require a prayer? A phone call? A meal? A visit? A ride? Some cash (if we have it)? The Bible calls us to wear several hats, especially if the friend is another Christian. Do we need to be an encourager or a server? Is there a burden to bear or a truth to be spoken in love? As a friend, do we need to admonish in order to restore a relationship? God calls us to many roles with our friends.

"Call me if there is anything I can do" is not a real offer of help. It puts the responsibility to take the initiative back on the one who needs help. They need a more specific offer if the situation is overwhelming. When our emotions kick in sometimes they overtake our common sense. Our friend may not even know what she needs. She will probably be open to almost any suggestion.

Recently, a woman in our church who has several children was going through a particularly difficult time. A friend offered to take the children for a few hours to give her a break. She didn't call so the friend offered again...and again... and again. As a good friend, she finally called her one Monday and said, "I can take your children either Friday or Saturday, choose which one you would like me to take them."

This phone call and the day off that followed allowed my friend a real break for a few hours. It was an act of kindness, service, encouragement, and love!

When Jonathan visited David in the wilderness, David was on the run, hiding from Saul as he sought to take David's life. Jonathan did not send a messenger asking what he could do to help. He showed up and offered encouragement in the Lord. It helped David.

Face Time
In our culture, it is extremely easy to sit in our sweat pants, pajamas, or yoga pants (depending on our age!) at our computers (or on our cell phones) and try to minister from afar. Not only am I struck by the truth of Jonathan traveling thirty miles into the wilderness to encourage David, I am convicted by a verse in Exodus 33. God was

instructing Moses about moving the Israelites into the Promised Land. Moses set up the tent of meeting outside the Israelite camp. When he, or anyone else, wanted to seek the Lord they would go to this tent to 'meet the Lord.'

Exodus 33:9-11 says, *When Moses entered the tent, the pillar of cloud would descend and stand at the entrance of the tent, and the LORD would speak with Moses. And when all the people saw the pillar of cloud standing at the entrance of the tent, all the people would rise up and worship, each at his tent door. Thus the LORD used to speak to Moses face to face, as a man speaks to his friend.*

God specifies that this friendly conversation was face to face. I do not know if He is saying they always have to be face to face, but it clearly says face-to -face contact happens in friendships! Sometimes I fear we are stopping short of going to our friends because, quite frankly, we are comfortable in our sweats, yoga pants, or pajamas in front of our computers. Are we being too lazy to get up and go to the side of a friend in need?

When a woman emails me about her husband being on her last nerve or that she is ready to scream over unkept promises, I have to make my best guess about what kind of emotion is behind her words. Is she being sarcastic or frustrated, or is she calling it quits? When I sit across from her and listen to her words, I can hear her tone of voice and see if it is mischief or anguish in her eyes. It is hard to discern her needs from the comfort of our own home, with only the sound of her voice, or the written words on an email or text message.

Being a good friend to someone in her hour of need brings a blessing as we follow God's instructions to love, admonish, and encourage a friend. Prayer will be required so God will direct us as we minister to her. Sacrifice will be required: it may cost us time, money, and emotional investment (and maybe taking off our comfy clothes to go to her side). We have to speak the truth in love if our friend is tempted to sin in response to her circumstances. A true, Christian friend will love at all times – in times of rejoicing and in times of mourning.

Being a friend will require action and discernment to direct us to take the right action. Have we been so affected by our culture we would rather Facebook message, text, or email to commiserate or celebrate with a friend, rather than show up and do it face to face?

11
Choosing Wisely

Whoever covers an offense seeks love, but he who repeats a matter separates close friends. Proverbs 17:9

One summer when our daughter was in her late teens she was working at a summer camp. We called her after the first couple of days and she was gleefully telling us about a young man she had met. When we got there to visit her the following week, we asked to meet him. She dismissed the question with, "Nah, you don't need to meet him." She went on to explain that in those few short days he had demonstrated an angry personality. She was not interested any longer. That was fine with us!

The Scriptures speak of friendships and offers sound wisdom about how we are treated and influenced by others.

One is a warning that we should not have anything to do with an angry person. Proverbs 22:24-25 states it clearly: *Make no friendship with a man given to anger, nor go with a wrathful man, lest you learn his ways and entangle yourself in a snare.*

If you are reading this and you are single – apply this to any man you might be considering marrying, not just female friends. Usually, if someone is this angry, she has other areas of emotion also out of control. As a friend, at first she may seem very devoted but later she may seem more controlling or too close. Beware of the angry person and try to point her to her need to resolve the anger. Angry friends can lead us down the same path affecting our attitudes of thanksgiving and selfishness. An angry woman wants things her way.

Another warning every woman needs to hear, and one the Bible repeatedly talks about, is our control of our words. I think there are so many verses about this topic that it seems clear God is emphasizing how big a problem it is.

- *Whoever covers an offense seeks love, but he who repeats a matter separates close friends.* Proverbs 17.9

- *A dishonest man spreads strife, and a whisperer separates close friends.* Proverbs 16.28

Whoever goes about slandering reveals secrets; therefore do not associate with a simple babbler. Proverbs 20.19

Gossips and babblers, whisperers and slanderers, anyone who puts other people down so she will look better is trouble. Do not associate with her. If she is a sister in the Lord you may need to tell her why!

Now, I do not know anyone who is not occasionally guilty of gossip or talking too much, including myself, I am sorry to say. These verses are talking about the person who makes a lifestyle of babbling. If you spend time with her, you know what kind of conversation you will have. You leave the time together feeling like you need a lengthy time of confession and a shower!

Here is the general rule in friendships. (Actually, this is true for all relationships, romantic, and business as well.) From 1 Corinthians 15:33, *Do not be deceived: Bad company ruins good morals.* If we want friends who will be positive biblical friends, we need to choose carefully those honoring God with their words and actions.

Carefully choosing friends is important for our own spiritual growth. Choose another woman who wants to love and serve the Lord. Do not choose for the wrong reasons – for what she can do for me. Do not choose one who is only interested in herself, who is angry, self-indulgent, or a gossiper or slanderer.

Let's stop here and look at our own hearts. By this standard, should someone seek you or me out as a friend?

The Bible commands us to love one another, serve one another, encourage one another, and admonish one another. We need to practice all of these with our friends, and we should expect them to practice these with us.

Friendship is a two-way street. We should give as much as we get.

Friend or Mentor

As Christian women there may be times when we are approached by a woman to be her "friend," when what she is really looking for is a mentor. Some friendships may be formed from a mentoring relationship but the kind of reciprocity found in a friendship is often not part of a mentoring relationship.

Though we may not choose to have an angry, selfish person, or a gossiper or slanderer for a friend, we may have one come to us about a mentoring relationship. A Christian woman caught in any one of these sins, who wants to seek God's guidance or an accountability partner to try to change her behavior, truly needs help. The Bible instructs us to bear one another's burdens and to teach.

A woman we mentor may not become a close friend though we spend concentrated time together. The opposite is also true, because we spend concentrated time together, and have the privilege of seeing God at work in her life, we may see change and become close friends.

I think of friendship with the women we mentor like the friendship we have with Jesus Christ. In John 15:15 Jesus is talking to His disciples. He has told them that after He leaves He will send the Holy Spirit. He tells them that He is the Vine and they are the branches. He calls them to abide in Him because, He says, *Apart from me you can do nothing.* He informs them that He is telling them these things so they will have His joy in them and that God is glorified when they bear much fruit. He tells them He loves them and encourages them to abide in that love.

In John 15:13-15 Jesus says these words, *Greater love has no one than this, that someone lay down his life for his friends. You are my friends if you do what I command you. No longer do I call you servants, for the servant does not know what his master is doing; but I have called you friends, for all that I have heard from my Father I have made known to you.*

Though we should never expect anyone to obey our commands, or expect that they can do nothing apart from us (in fact we want them to grow so they lean more and more on Christ), the friendship that Jesus displays for those who follow Him should inform the way that we show friendship to the women we mentor. When Jesus gave these words He was a walking, talking, human being. He could not possibly be a "BFF" (that is, best friend forever) to everyone who was present to hear these words. This is true even if it was only the twelve disciples. As a human He was limited by the same factors we are.

He befriended people by loving them by teaching them what God the Father had made known to Him (John 15:15). He befriended them by loving them enough to lay down His life for them (John 15:13). He befriended them by speaking the truth about their behavior (John 15:2). He befriended them by teaching about the expectations of God (John 15:3, 4, 8, 10). In John 15:11 Jesus tells them what is in it for them when they show they are His friends by obeying His commands. He set the example by obeying the commands of His Father. *These things I have spoken to you, that my joy may be in you, and that your joy may be full (* John 15:11).

Whether we are in a reciprocal relationship with a faithful friend, showing friendship as Jesus did by sacrificing time and effort, or ministering to a woman in need of spiritual growth, teaching her to be more like Jesus, we will be more like Him.

Mentoring is an intentional way to come alongside and teach another what the Father has taught us through His Son Jesus Christ. We might do this one on one or with a small group of women. Our friendliness to them may not ever evolve into a reciprocal, close and personal, friendship; however, we can be a faithful friend to the women we mentor by following the example set for us by the best Friend we have ever had.

In many respects Jonathan's friendship with David was a picture of Jesus' friendship with us. Like Christ comes to us while we are in the crisis of sin, Jonathan went to David when he was struggling and lost in a wilderness. Jonathan made covenants with David as Jesus has made a covenant with us in our salvation (Hebrews 12:24). Jesus sacrificed His life for us as Jonathan sacrificed his royal position for David. Jesus speaks the truth to us, even when it is hard to believe, just as Jonathan did for David.

Jonathan was intentional as he ministered to David in his times of trouble. Jesus is intentional with us as He has, and continues to, minister to us in our sinful condition. Whether in a personal friendship or a mentoring relationship, our goal is to be more like Jesus

12
Marching Orders

But be doers of the word, and not hearers only, deceiving yourselves.
James 1:22

God has shown us great grace by leaving us His Word with clear commands, not wishy-washy instructions. James 1:22 (above) clearly tells us we are to do what the Word of God says, not just to read it or hear it preached. God calls us to action.

In Titus 2:3-5 we find understanding of what He wants us as women to know and live as a part of our faith in Jesus Christ. He left us a plan for teaching the next generation how to live peaceful, joyful, even happy lives, free from strife! (Okay, not perfectly happy, but with less strife and more peace.) Here it is again:

Older women likewise are to be reverent in behavior, not slanderers or slaves to much wine. They are to teach what is good, and so train the young women to love their husbands and children, to be self-controlled, pure, working at home, kind, and submissive to their own husbands, that the word of God may not be reviled. Titus 2:3-5

God communicates to us in these three verses what we need to be and to teach so *His name will not be reviled.* A reviled name is a name detested by or despicable to others. The King James version says, *so that His name will not be blasphemed.* In the mentoring relationship, we are to teach the one we mentor to know and honor God's Word and in so-doing also honor His name. Through biblical instruction we are trying to prevent their reviling, or causing others to revile, and blaspheme God's reputation. If our counsel to them is not biblical, although we teach as if it is, and thus it reaps few benefits, then we cause God's Word to be blasphemed, hated, despised, and disrespected.

This is why God starts with the behavior of the older woman. It has to begin there. We are to *"be reverent in behavior, not slanderers, nor slaves to much wine."* Many women, especially new believers, read these words and loosely interpret them to say, "no fun allowed." Is that what God really said?

Heart Exam

I take these words to mean God wants us to examine our own hearts and lives before we begin to think we can speak biblical truth into someone else's.

An older woman told me about a Bible Study she had joined. She came to saving faith in Jesus Christ later in life. In fact, she had been watching as two grown Christian daughters and their families demonstrated living their faith in front of her for several years. She had been a career woman, so her daughters' "stay at home Mom" and "submissive" roles in their marriages were offensive to her at first. But, as her own faith and Bible knowledge grew, and she watched the harmony and happiness her daughters and their families were experiencing, God gave her a hunger to learn to love her own husband this way. What better place to go than to a Bible Study with several older women so she could hear how they do it?

Without naming names or pointing fingers, she said that most of the women in the Bible Study openly criticized and disrespected their husbands during the discussions. One or two would mock their husbands without any correction from the leader. She was so disappointed. I found her description heartbreaking. Some Christian women seem to have little or no concern for whether or not their words, their actions, and their attitudes, honor their husbands or their God.

Please consider a few verses in which God has left us clear instructions. These are instructions we should not just teach to younger women but also follow ourselves.

- *Wives, submit to your own husbands, as to the Lord.* Ephesians 5:22
- *Now as the church submits to Christ, so also wives should submit in everything to their husband.* Ephesians 5:24
- *However, let each one of you love his wife as himself, and let the wife see that she respects her husband.* Ephesians 5:33
- *But I want you to understand that the head of every man is Christ, the head of a wife is her husband, and the head of Christ is God.* 1 Corinthians 11:3

- *For the wife does not have authority over her own body, but the husband does. Likewise the husband does not have authority over his own body, but the wife does.* 1 Corinthians 7:4
- *The husband should give to his wife her conjugal rights, and likewise the wife to her husband.* 1 Corinthians 7:3

Though these were older women, believers in the Lord Jesus Christ, they were not demonstrating reverent behavior. I was grateful this woman was not thrown off track. She sought help from those she witnessed in the church living in marital harmony.

Reverent behavior shows respect for the Word of God all the time, not just on Sunday morning. The woman who is reverent, ready, and able to teach what is good will examine her own heart before she starts. Below are a few questions for you to use as a tool for self-evaluation. If you fall short, do not despair, but remember we serve a forgiving and Holy God. He will, as 1 John 1:9 says, *forgive confessed sin and cleanse us from all unrighteousness.*

1. Do you read, study, and meditate on the Word of God regularly? (Daily is great, regularly is good).
2. Do you desire to keep the commands of God, starting with the Ten Commandments?
3. Does your life set a good example? Would others say you revere and respect the Word of God from the way you live?
4. Do you speak well of your husband, to him and about him to others? Do you show him respect?
5. Do you believe and live the truth that children are a gift from God?
6. Is your home a place where others are welcomed and would be comfortable?
7. Are your family's needs your highest priority?
8. Are you raising, or have you raised, your children to love and serve the Lord, even if they have chosen not to follow Him? (If you have come to know the Lord late in life this may not be something you were able to do.)

9. Are you regularly attending worship services and serving the church?
10. Are others witnessing you living a life of purity in your marriage, in entertainment, in what you read?
11. Are you a slanderer or a gossip?
12. Are you drinking too much alcohol? Are you getting drunk?

Obviously, we will not be perfect in all of these things. Our intentions should be to serve the Lord, to love Him, and to set an example of godly living. These questions are one way to start to look at our own lives. Should we be mentoring someone younger right now or should we first be focusing on growth in our own faith, getting rid of laziness or sinful living in our own lives?

Teaching What Is Good

Titus 2:1 says, *But as for you, teach what accords with sound doctrine.* In verse 3 Paul, in his letter to Titus, addresses older women "likewise." He is saying, just as for the men he spoke to in verses one and two, women are being held to this same doctrinal standard of teaching. He is expanding on this initial instruction. *"Teach what is good."* "What is good" and "sound doctrine" go hand in hand. The verse implies that when we teach what is good (doctrinally sound) it will train the younger women.

In chapter 6 we discussed several ways we teach and train (formally, informally, by example, etc.). Some of it is very intentional and calls for teaching in a formal setting. Other times we don't even know we are teaching because others are watching how we respond or act in certain situations. Sometimes the Lord gives us a surprise opportunity to speak truth into the life of another woman (a Divine appointment). We need to be ready.

Titus 2:1 requires us to live a doctrinally sound faith all the time. The way we speak about our husbands, the way we speak to our children, the books our neighbors see sitting around the house, the service we offer the Lord, will all give some clue of what we regard as "good" and they will learn from these examples. We will face temptation, maybe we will occasionally fall; but at the very least we should aspire to follow this ideal.

Holiness is a standard set for us in the scriptures. Just as the women who criticized their husbands in the Bible Study set a poor example, un-holiness should not be seen in us (without repentance!). Those older women in the Bible study had no idea this woman's goal was to learn to love her husband from a biblical perspective. She assumed this would be a place to see and hear the examples she could follow. It was disappointing, but the Lord used it as a lesson on what not to do in public regarding her husband,

A mentor must, first and foremost, be a woman of character and clearly demonstrate a desire to live according to the Word of God. She must be a pray-er as well as a mentor. Some may think it selfish to pray for ourselves daily and even first. What do we have to offer if we have not asked God to show us our sin, to lead us on a path of holiness, and give us the strength to fight the desires of the flesh and the temptations of the world? How will we teach others a holiness we have not yet asked for ourselves?

The Bible tells us to be holy because God is holy. Holiness sets us apart from the world, we are not to live like those in the world. As we intentionally set out to influence the next generation of women to live holy lives before their own families, we must test ours:

- Is there a level of holiness others will see?
- Are we responding to hardship and joy just like the world?
- Are we thankful in all circumstances?
- Are we bearing fruit?

Take the following two verses and compare your thoughts and actions to their instruction. They set a standard to judge our own holiness.

So, whether you eat or drink, or whatever you do, do all to the glory of God. 1 Corinthians 10:31

Finally, brothers, whatever is true, whatever is honorable, whatever is just, whatever is pure, whatever is lovely, whatever is commendable, if there is any excellence, if there is anything worthy of praise, think about these things. Philippians 4:8

True, honorable, just, pure, lovely, commendable, excellent, and worthy of praise. All to the glory of God. Do these words describe the things we do, the people we are in relationship with, or the way we think and entertain ourselves? Does everything we do bring honor and glory to God? How about in relation to the kind of living Titus 2:3-5 calls us to?

Every older woman in the church can teach "what is good" by the example we set in our own lives or in a focused mentoring relationship regarding the following six areas of life:

- Loving our husbands
- Loving our children
- Being self-controlled
- Living in purity
- Working at home
- Submitting to our husbands

Living these ourselves is hard enough. How are we to teach them? In the next section, we will look at each one separately, starting with "You can't fix stupid."

Section 3: The Mentoring

13
Intentional Training For Wives

Train the younger women to love their husband. Titus 2:4

Do you remember Diane (from chapter 6) who said, "You can't fix stupid"?

This was a very strong statement to make about her husband at our first meeting.

Diane said it again the next time we met. She was in a difficult marriage and seemed to be trying to make it seem as if she understood it. She did, in a "husband-bashing" kind of way. Inexplicably, she had learned this saying from a Christian friend who was also in a difficult marriage. Trying to portray their husbands as incapable of turning things around seemed to have become a coping mechanism. Diane was feeling hopeless about her marriage. She couldn't see these were not helpful words. Not helpful for her hopelessness, or for her marriage.

How was Diane going to learn to love her husband? (Only through the grace of God and the power of His Holy Spirit.)

And how was I going to teach or encourage her? (Only through the grace of God and the power of the Holy Spirit.)

Couples often start practicing attitudes and behaviors early in their relationships that go for years without being challenged. Some of these may require some retraining to offer a new, biblical, perspective on the part of the husband and/or the wife, and the role of God. Adopting this new perspective will hopefully change their attitudes or behaviors accordingly. The goals, of course, are a God-honoring marriage, children reared to love and serve Him, and peace in the household.

This may mean showing a new wife, or a wife in a difficult marriage, a verse like Philippians 2:3, *but in humility, count others as more significant than yourselves.* It may take pointing out that this kind of humility applies to how they treat their husbands, teaching them how important it is to respect their husbands. Every woman needs to know how to speak up to her husband, to let him know what she is thinking, sometimes, maybe even that she does think. She also needs to express those thoughts with an attitude and tone of voice communicating respect for him. Isn't this how we want to communicate to everyone? Hard words do not have to be harsh words.

Diane, convinced she could "not fix stupid," was facing her marital problems with an attitude of defeat before she started. We attempted to look at verses talking about the sovereignty of God, His love for His children, and assurance that nothing is impossible with Christ. She stopped using the expression (at least around me) but I do not think she became convinced that her husband could change. I had   to remember that only God could change her heart attitude.

Women need to understand the man's God-given role as leader of the family and respect him in his role. Respect conveys love for a husband. Patience will be a necessary part of our conversations as we teach them how to wait. Their timing and their husband's timing may (probably will) be different. We may need to teach a young wife to encourage and build up her husband as he steps out and tries to "climb the corporate ladder." If his own wife is not supportive, but is instead, critical and demeaning, he will be torn down and his "climb to the top" will be thwarted. He will be affected at work and at home, even in the church as he might consider God's call into leadership. Proverbs 31:11-12 speak to the benefit a godly wife can be to her husband, *The heart of her husband trusts in her, and he will have no lack of gain. She does him good, and not harm, all the days of her life.*

Women are a powerful force in the marriage. In the movie, "My Big Fat Greek Wedding" there is a woman who tells her daughter, "the man may be the head of the marriage, but the wife is the neck, and she can turn him any way she wants." As women, we can be a powerful, positive force by loving our husbands as the Bible calls us to do. We can also be a powerful negative force if we fail to respect them, as we are instructed to do. One of the ways we can teach this concept is to model it with our own husbands in front of the young women around us.

The instructions for the older woman to teach the younger include not only Titus 2 about loving their husbands, but Ephesians 5:22 which tells us we are to submit (a later chapter unto itself) to our husbands, and Proverbs 21:9 which says, *It is better to live in a corner of the housetop than in a house shared with a quarrelsome wife.* Add to those the instructions we all have to love our neighbors as ourselves and to love one another, serve one another, admonish one another, and encourage one another, and we can see many ways to love our husbands.

As in many situations calling us to teach, often a question to the younger woman may be a better approach than a rebuke or correction. For instance, the third time Diane gave me the, "you can't fix stupid" remark, as gently as I know how, I asked her if she thought those words honored her husband or God. She knew they did not. We talked about honoring God, who created her husband in His image. A conversation about exactly what she was trying to communicate by the "stupid" insult came from this discussion. I wondered out loud how much faith it proclaimed in the ability of Christ to do *more than we can ask or imagine?*

Do you see the series of questions? From the statement, " can't fix stupid," Diane and I were able to discuss:

- How does this honor God or your husband?
- What is it that you are intending to communicate when you say it?
- How much faith is behind the statement?

These questions led to more productive conversation as she considered exactly what she was trying to say and how it conveyed what was really in her heart. Questions can cause a woman to probe her own heart, whereas accusations might have caused her to become defensive to protect it.

This particular lady, and it seems there are many like her out there, was living in an especially difficult, verbally abusive, marriage situation. These are challenging and do require some extra attention and a close look at the Scriptures. Unfortunately many of these women, even in verbally or physically abusive situations, have been given some real simplistic advice for their very complicated situations. On face value it might appear the Bible does not address these issues directly. Giving a woman in this situation the standard "submit" or "love him more" answers is basically putting a tiny Band-Aid on a six inch gash while it is bleeding profusely!

When we mentor about marriage we tend to look only at the verses in the Scriptures speaking directly to marriage. We look for the words "marriage," "husband", "wife", when we seek verses about how to approach the subject. But, assuming we are talking about a Christian couple, there are many verses confronting the sin of both husband and wife to apply to abusive situations.

- *The LORD tests the righteous, but his soul hates the wicked and the one who loves violence.* Psalm 11:5
- *The prudent sees danger and hides himself, but the simple go on and suffer for it.* Proverbs 27:12
- *But now you must put them all away: anger, wrath, malice, slander, and obscene talk from your mouth.* Colossians 3:8
- *Husbands, love your wives, and do not be harsh with them.* Colossians 3:19
- *Be angry and do not sin; do not let the sun go down on your anger.* Ephesians 4:26
- *Likewise, husbands, live with your wives in an understanding way, showing honor to the woman as the weaker vessel, since they are heirs with you of the grace of life, so that your prayers may not be hindered.* 1 Peter 3:7

For a married man not to keep or obey these instructions from God is sin. Allowing a brother to remain in sin without a warning, is sin for us. A wife needs to protect herself and her children from an angry, abusive man. When we encourage an abused woman to speak up about the sin in her home, she is loving her husband by helping him to see that what he is doing is sin, ripe for God's judgment. This is a scary thought for many women in difficult marriages. They may need the support of a mentor telling her she is not wrong to seek help if the marriage is abusive.

James 5:19-20 say, *My brothers, if anyone among you wanders from the truth and someone brings him back, let him know that whoever brings back a sinner from his wandering will save his soul from death and will cover a multitude of sins.* We must teach wives to approach husbands without anger and in love. Ephesians 4:25 tells us to *speak the truth in love.*

One way to do that is to teach a woman to approach her husband with questions instead of accusations. Some questions that may help her to bring up the topic to her husband might be:

- *Do you think our relationship pleases God? (Rather than the accusation that, "God hates the way you treat me!"*
- *I think we need help. Would you be willing to talk to a marriage counselor with me? (Rather than, "You will go see a marriage counselor or I am outta here!" This is not to say that a woman in this situation might not eventually get to the point where she has to insist.)*
- *Can we talk about how to discipline the children so they see us as united on what we allow? (Rather than, "You can't say that to them!" or "Don't ever talk to the kids like that again!")*
- *Could we please have this conversation when I am calmer and have had some time to think about it? (Rather than blowing up angrily, walking out on it or saying nothing, and having the other party believe that everything is fine because there was no argument.)*

Questions do not always give us the answer we are looking for. They will often, though, give us the information we need, without creating a bigger battle. An accusation is disrespectful, when a question, spoken in a humble tone of voice, offers respect. (This is a principle to be applied even for the "good" marriage with its day to day complaints.)

In Matthew 18 the Bible gives us a systematic way to confront the sin of a man who is sinning against us. If he refuses to listen when first approached by his wife, she should get one or two witnesses and confront him again. If he continues to refuse to acknowledge the sin or, if there is no resolution in sight, the wife may take her complaint to the church. This may be a Pastor or to the elders at first, so her husband can be confronted by godly leaders about his sin. I have found it's not unusual for the wife to need the presence of a close friend or mentor to support her in order to follow through. She may be intimidated by the men of leadership.

Many evangelical Christian churches have a reputation (earned by some, unfortunately) for failing to hear the complaint of an abused wife. If her husband is well known and liked in the congregation, or he is a leader in the church, there may be resistance to believing her. Many of these women go outside the church to local authorities if the abuse is physical or to a biblical counselor if she feels safe enough to stay in the home.

Many churches are attempting to solve this problem by working with a counselor on staff or a contracted therapist outside the church.

Many women find that a husband's sin can be difficult to expose. We are taught to protect our husbands (which we want to do anytime we can), to love them at all costs, and to only, ever speak well of them. Many women fear approaching the church with the truth of what is going on at home. Sometimes, the woman creates part of the problem by making an idol of having the perfect Christian marriage or family. She does not want anyone to know. She says nothing, or minimizes the issues, until the problems are so great all she wants is out. Unfortunately, because she pretends that all is well for so long, it is hard for the church to believe there are problems when she finally does speak up.

The Bible warns us not to let the circumstances get so bad. God *wants* to deliver us from the hands of evil and the oppression holding us down.

- *LORD, you hear the desire of the afflicted; you will strengthen their heart; you will incline your ear to do justice to the fatherless and the oppressed, so that man who is of the earth may strike terror no more.* Psalm 10:17-18
- *I know that the LORD will maintain the cause of the afflicted, and will execute justice for the needy.* Psalm 140:12
- *... discretion will watch over you, understanding will guard you, delivering you from the way of evil, from men of perverted speech, who forsake the paths of uprightness to walk in the ways of darkness, who rejoice in doing evil and delight in the perverseness of evil, men whose paths are crooked, and who are devious in their ways.* Proverbs 2:11-15

- *With his mouth the godless man would destroy his neighbor, but by knowledge the righteous are delivered.* Proverbs 11:9

Women living in abusive marriages need to be taught to pray about it, of course, but also to speak up about it. In Ephesians 5:11 Paul says, *Take no part in the unfruitful works of darkness, but instead expose them.* He is warning the Ephesians about all kinds of sin and uncleanness, telling them not to participate in any of it. Anytime a husband and wife are living two separate lives, the one they allow the church to see and the one they live at home, something is wrong. If there is a darkness shrouding what is happening at home, it needs to be exposed, especially if it is abusive to the wife and/or children. (This is just as true if the wife is the abuser.)

If the marriage is still young, there is a better chance they will be able to reconcile with some help. If the woman has been in the marriage for many years and has silently, or unheard, hung in there, she may be at the end of her rope. The sooner these problems are faced head on in a godly way, the greater the likelihood there will not be a divorce. Both partners have to be willing.

As a mentor we may face Christian women who have learned from a very young age that God hates divorce, and He does. Matthew 19:6 says, *So they are no longer two but one flesh. What therefore God has joined together, let not man separate.* Because of this, some Christians find it difficult to tell a woman to separate herself from her husband to protect herself and her children. This is not always a step toward divorce, but an attempt to begin the process of reconciliation and safely address the issues without fear of harm. Look at these verses from the Scriptures:

- *Guard me, O LORD, from the hands of the wicked; preserve me from violent men, who have planned to trip up my feet.* Psalm 140:4
- *A man of great wrath will pay the penalty, for if you deliver him, you will only have to do it again.* Proverbs 19:19

Sometimes God will do a great work in a marriage where separation took place while the couple sought help. There are many biblical counselors who can point a couple to God's view of their situation and how He can direct them. When this is the case, I am happy to come alongside and encourage a wife by studying the Scriptures, holding up her arms in the battle, and providing encouragement any way I can.

In cases of verbal or physical abuse, I count myself unqualified to be the primary help and refer to a biblical counselor or pastor. Remember back in Chapter 6 when we talked about interviewing and setting boundaries in the mentoring relationship? For me, this is one of those red flag areas. The woman who marries an abuser, and the abuser, both have deep spiritual and emotional problems greater than my abilities. It is important to know our limits as mentors. I still meet with her to mentor and encourage her spiritual growth and dependence on the Lord, but sometimes I know they need more than I can offer. (It may take time to convince the abused spouse of her need for professional help. Some live in denial of the seriousness of their problems.)

Generally speaking, counselors are not as available as a mentor. They work certain hours and rarely can spend a lot of time beyond the scheduled appointment with a client. I do not feel personally qualified to tell a woman how long she should stay in a marriage or if she should separate (unless there is serious abuse). But, I can listen to her when she needs to tell someone what is happening in a crisis. It will be helpful for a mentor to have set up some guidelines for the relationship. Do we have time to meet regularly but not take phone calls because of work or home situations? Is an occasional phone call acceptable to you? Is she willing to have you call her back at a convenient time or pray for her and talk when you get together? Each mentor has to decide her own limits and establish them. If they are established, talked about early on, it is easier to stick to them in a more difficult time.

In God's goodness and grace to the mentor, not all women who need to learn how to love their husbands are in abusive situations! Most women need to be encouraged to be intentional about their marriage relationships. They need the reminder of what it means to be submissive (not a doormat), and how to show respect.

Perhaps you live in a marriage where you learned these lessons and can direct a younger woman. If not, there are plenty of Bible studies on marriage, even DVD series available as tools for teaching. If you have not done things biblically, perhaps your bad example can be a good teacher! Humbly admit wrong attitudes and unbiblical thinking, and where it led so the consequences of these things can be clearly taught.

For fun, as I was writing, I "tweeted" (on Twitter) that I was writing about teaching younger women to love their husbands and asked if they had any suggestions about what to include. The first one gave me a link to her blog. In it she describes her hectic life with three children who go to bed at 7:30 PM. She and her husband assumed an early bedtime would give them "connect time." They were wrong, they both were so busy that they still continued to feel disconnected. They scheduled Wednesday nights as a "date night." They do not leave home but she gave a list of what they attend to. Here are her own words, "Wednesday night is sacredly protected for us. To put **us** first. To pray. To rub feet. To make plans. To dream. To pursue oneness. To build into our marriage. To put our titles of Mommy and Daddy on the back-burner to remember we are also *Husband and Wife*."[6]

The second one said to tell the younger women (of which she is one) "It is a choice daily. Not because of what he does, but because of what Christ has done for you. Christ taught us true love."

What a great place to start. If we point young women to Christ, to remembering how sacrificial His love is for us, how compassionate He was to people when they were in pain, and how He served rather than looking to be served, then they will see a blueprint for marriage. Also good to teach is that God will use our marriages to draw us closer to Him, in dependence on Him, and not each other, as we learn to obey His Word.

If you choose to do a biblical study on marriage, these truths are often covered. A mentor can also point to these truths in conversations about what is happening at home. If a wife is complaining that her husband is inattentive, I might ask her how attentive she has been to

---

[6] www.amandalynndesigns.com

him? It is important to look at the fact that we cannot change another person, only ourselves. The more a wife can see her own shortcomings, and correct them, the more responsive her husband is likely to be (in a healthy marriage).

Some of the women we mentor will be easier than others to teach to love their husbands. Especially difficult is the one coming in already convinced she married an unlovable man. Easier is the one who comes in teachable, with a heart to change, with a desire to do things God's way, through the power of the Holy Spirit in them. She can change and she will grow. Great blessings will come to her. Her husband and their children and their children's children will be the beneficiaries. What a legacy to take part in for a family!

14
Intentionally Love The Children

If you then, who are evil, know how to give good gifts to your children, how much more will your Father who is in heaven give good things to those who ask him! Matthew 7:11

Train the younger women to love their children...Titus 2:4

"I love my children, I love my children, I love my children…!" I can't tell you how many times as my children were growing up I would repeat this mantra – to remind myself. I used it when they upset me with typical childish behavior. I knew I should not punish them but it was irritating, nonetheless. I recognize now my irritation was from being robbed of my comfort in the moment and I wanted it back! A mentor would have been great to have to help me parent!

At the same time, I can also see I idolized my children early on. After my husband and I became Christians the Lord intervened and showed us that we needed to be more consistent in parenting. I would start to walk away from an argument, giving up on convincing my son of something, and God would remind me I could not let the subject go. He had to understand what he needed to do or that we had the authority to tell him what to do. We were able to see the need, for the sake of those little idols who would one day become adults, to prioritize God and provide consistent discipline, which gave needed security to our children.

Many of us older parents who did not know the Lord or the scriptures when our children were small feel like we failed our children in the way we parented them. Or maybe we went into the marriage as a Christian, expecting to parent as our Christian parents did, only to find that our spouse sees parenting quite differently. Sometimes prioritizing peace in the marriage leaves active, intentional parenting behind. As a mentor we may be able to help a woman approach her husband in love and respect to talk about these differences. We can also encourage a mother who thinks she has been doing it wrong to institute changes that will prioritize God in her family and the discipline of older children.

Other Christian parents are affected by the culture which, in many ways, has become so fearful of abuse (which is a terrible thing to do to a child) that they have opted for little to no discipline. This extreme leaves us with children not raised to love and fear the Lord and who think the world revolves around them.

What does a woman, who is a child of God, need to be taught in order to love her children so they will grow up in the discipline and instruction of the Lord (Ephesians 6:4)? How does one who did not do it for her own children teach the next generation to do it? Only with help, and the good news is that God left us help.

It is in His Word!

Consider Before You Start

As hungry as she might be, as eager as she might be to learn what God's Word says, a mother is a busy person. One of the most difficult parts of mentoring a mother of young children is her schedule. It may take some willing flexibility from you as her mentor to meet on her schedule. It might be best in the early afternoon when children are napping or early in the morning or after they go to bed, when Dad is home to care for them.

These mothers are appreciative people in general. Many are seeking the advice and counsel of a godly, older woman who has already been through this part of her life. They want to raise children for the Lord. Many of them are confused about how. We can use a Bible study, our own experiences, or we can use examples from someone else's experience. What we want is to convey the importance of the work parents do, and the advantage for a child who is raised to love and serve the Lord. Just like the intentionality of our mentoring relationship, we want to stress their own intentionality in how they approach parenting.

The Word of God has a lot to say about childrearing. Look at what God says about raising children in the Proverbs, about character traits, and discipline. In Colossians 3 the Lord tells us what character traits are to be eliminated and what ones to put on. Ephesians 6 speaks about the need for children to honor their parents. As a mentor we can discuss rewards and punishments, discipline versus abuse, and how parents can model these traits as well as teach them. All with Biblical support.

There are many books written about parenting and many Bible studies available, but…please remember not every book in a Christian bookstore or with a biblical sounding title is written from a biblical perspective. As trusted "older women" we are responsible to choose our resources wisely. Someone on Facebook posted an article sounding very biblical but the blogger's bottom line on discipline was that if you extend grace you will discipline without ever getting physical. She felt all any child ever needed was a good "mommy talking to." This is not in agreement with the Scriptures.

Today's young mother may come with many questions. The world has thrown out scriptural truths and clouded the minds of new parents, even believers. The culture we live in has devalued children by accepting abortions. Families, inside and outside of the church, seem to range from emphasizing the comfort and convenience of the parents above the needs or the life of the child, to the family that completely indulges the children regardless of cost or eventual consequences of idolizing the children. Every Christian parent needs to be pointed to the scriptures for priorities in parenting and family life.

As we meet and talk with mothers we can share what we have experienced, the good and the bad. They can learn from our mistakes as well as from our successes, if we are willing to humble ourselves and tell them that we did not do it all right.

There are certain freedoms regarding discipline that have been taken from us.

Spank your child in the grocery store, and you may have a visit from the civil authorities because of your "abuse." Physical abuse of any child is wrong and should be stopped (preferably, never started). God would agree, in Psalm 11:5 He says, *The LORD tests the righteous, but his soul hates the wicked and the one who loves violence.* Discipline and violence are not related. Discipline cannot be compromised. Children love and need to know their boundaries. There is security in rules, not legalism. Guidelines give them standards to live by so they understand when they step over the line and are headed for trouble.

We recently went to Dutch Wonderland (an amusement park in Lancaster, PA designed for young children) with our two grandchildren who were three and five years old. This was their first experience in an amusement park. Since I was writing this book and my husband and I were teaching a parenting class at our church, I was paying particular attention to interactions between parents and their children.

Amusement parks are exhausting for a young child. For some there is so much stimulation it is hard for them to enjoy the day without at least one meltdown. I watched as a couple of pre-school boys who were not getting their way slapped their Mom or Dad. I saw a child kicking and screaming because he did not want to be in line for the ride, he wanted to be on it. These were demanding children. One little guy, obviously pushed to his limit, was so tired all he could do was cry. These may be adorable children under normal circumstances.

Early in the day our own granddaughter was whining because we were not at the ride she wanted to ride. In my own mind I was wondering what her problem was. We hadn't even gotten through the first hour! My daughter had the wisdom to understand her child had no idea what her day would look like. She looked her right in the eyes and explained we expected to be there for many hours so we would get to the roller coaster she had seen, but right now it made sense to do things in some order. The lesson learned for me was that the child who is prepared for her day will be better behaved.

(Now, if I have an opportunity, when I hear a family with young children say they are going to an amusement park, I tell them to prepare the children before they get there. It might make the day go more smoothly.)

As the day went on I realized many of the children there had not received preparation from their parents, no explanation of how things would work for the day (as ours had not before it became obvious to their mother they needed it). Talking to our children about what is going to happen can relieve a lot of stress and anxiety (which I had forgotten all about with our own grandchildren). Talk to them and there will be fewer surprises and fewer "meltdowns."

For a mother who has a child who doesn't like changes or surprises, this is a great lesson to teach her. Some parents fail to recognize their own children would respond better if prepared for the events they are heading into. Some peace may be brought to a family who learns to tell children what to expect. It is surprising how well, even a very young child, will understand when they hear the expectations or the plan for a day or an event.

One of the first lessons a young mother needs to learn about how to love her children is that the Bible's way is better than the world's way. When we do things the world's way, we may end up with disrespectful kids slapping us in an amusement park. When we listen to the instruction to discipline and teach the Word of God to our children, not just to hide it in their hearts, but to do what it says (James 1:22), we are more likely to have content, well-adjusted children who can interact with others in the world. Though we need to teach that there are never guarantees with children, we know children will be better off when they are raised as the Lord has designed for them to be raised. Isaiah 55:9 says, *For as the heavens are higher than the earth, so are my ways higher than your ways and my thoughts than your thoughts.*

Eight Biblical Parenting Principles

Relying on the Scriptures for our parenting education, there are several principles we can pass on to a young mother.

The first one is: Children will suffer because of the sin of their parents. Numbers 14:18 says, *The LORD is slow to anger and abounding in steadfast love, forgiving iniquity and transgression, but he will by no means clear the guilty, visiting the iniquity of the fathers on the children, to the third and the fourth generation.*

If a mother has a besetting sin, a sin having more control over her than she has over it, she needs to be aware that the consequences of her sin will affect her children. As God deals with her on her sin, so her children will also suffer the consequences. This is especially true if the sin is one of infidelity in marriage or even disrespect or an unloving attitude toward her husband (their father). If she fails to teach her children a proper respect for the father because she is always putting him down in front of them, they will all suffer. The fifth commandment says, *Honor your father and your mother, that your days may be long in the land that the LORD your God is giving you*

(Exodus 20:12). Children learn this honor from the way parents treat each other. If we want life to go well for our children, to have long lives in the land, then we have to model respect for their fathers and teach the mothers to do so, as well.

A second principle is: The marriage needs to be a higher priority than the children. A child's security is greatly increased when there is no fear or doubt about the marriage of their parents. Our son had a friend in high school who was very insecure. She once said to him she wasn't even sure her parents *liked* each other! She lived in doubt about the security of her home.

In the U.S. culture in recent years it seems to have become more and more acceptable to prioritize the children, *their* schedules, *their* sports, *their* social lives. Parents are so protective, they are afraid to let the child suffer some natural consequences of not completing work or missing a sporting event because of poor behavior or academics. The norm has become for parents to cover for their kids. The general rule is no consequences, no change.

By placing priority on the marriage rather than making idols of the children, the children benefit as adults.

Number three: Worshiping the Lord is a higher priority to our family than being at a game on Sunday morning. Or, that the character trait we are working on in that child by missing a game (or practice) is more important to us than whether or not the team wins the game. Consider these verses from Psalm 102:18-22:

Let this be recorded for a generation to come, so that a people yet to be created may praise the LORD: that he looked down from his holy height; from heaven the LORD looked at the earth, to hear the groans of the prisoners, to set free those who were doomed to die, that they may declare in Zion the name of the LORD, and in Jerusalem his praise, when peoples gather together, and kingdoms, to worship the LORD.

Because of God's rescue of us, we must teach the next generation to praise Him. Any compromise on this should be made with the world, not with our worship of the One who has saved us from an eternity in Hell and to service for Him. Serving God includes raising our children to love and fear Him. When our compromise is with the worship of the Lord rather than the distractions of the world, we teach the child what is more important. Baseball, softball, football, soccer, lacrosse, dance, instrumental music practice, whatever we allow children to place over the worship of the Ruler of the universe teaches a child he, or his activity, is of greater importance than the Lord.

In our sports and activity driven youth culture today it can take a lot of conviction and courage for parents to stand up to a coach and explain our desire to serve the Lord over the team.

The fourth principle to teach a young woman about how to love her children is: Follow the biblical prescription to teach them the Word of God. God is pretty specific about this being a parental responsibility.

And these words that I command you today shall be on your heart. You shall teach them diligently to your children, and shall talk of them when you sit in your house, and when you walk by the way, and when you lie down, and when you rise. You shall bind them as a sign on your hand, and they shall be as frontlets between your eyes. You shall write them on the doorposts of your house and on your gates. Deuteronomy 6:6-9

Similar instructions are repeated in Deuteronomy 11.

These efforts are to be intentional. Pointing a child to the laws of the Lord is the loving thing to do. They will protect him. They will direct him. Learning to obey them will also bring blessing and peace. But, there is so much more to this command.

We must also teach a mother of young children that she needs to motivate her children to want to obey the Lord. She can do this by remembering to include in her teaching the love of God, the goodness, and the mercy of God, not only His justice. Why would children want to follow God if all they ever hear are the "rules?" What about pointing out the times when we see His goodness, His kindness, His generosity, and His glory?

Children need to understand who God is through His creation, learning to be attentive to the beauty of His creation surrounding them, being aware of some of the great gifts He has given them or their family in general, understanding that He is the One who has gifted them with spiritual gifts and talents. God is so much more than a God of rules. He is the Almighty, Most Holy, the greatest Giver of good there is. Even a young child can learn how great God is and how faithful He will be to them when parents consciously teach them all day long. As parents, we can train ourselves and our children to see God in everything – and talk about it.

I was talking to a young mother recently about her discipline with regard to her children's school work. She told me how she repeatedly explains how God hates disobedience. I asked her if she had ever shown them the verses in Deuteronomy about the blessings for obedience. We looked them up in Deuteronomy 11 so she could find them to show her children.

There are many resources where we can easily look for and find what the Bible says about a particular area of life. I have found www.biblegateway.com to be a great resource that allows you to do individual word searches (and much more). I entered "obey" and "blessing" in the search box. It gave me many verses to consider.

The fifth principle to convey as we teach mothers to live by the Law of the Lord is: Adults of this world are just as dependent on the sacrifice of Christ, the renewing of the mind that comes through faith in Him, and His mercy, forgiveness and grace, as the children. Children need to know, from the example of the adults in their homes, that perfection is not attainable. Sharing is hard, loving all the time is hard, and forgiving others as God has forgiven us can be hard. But, through the power of His Holy Spirit, we can be constantly growing, improving, and accepted by the Lord as righteous, because of Christ. A child needs to see that we, as their parents, must rely on Christ, just as they must.

The sixth principle is: Start to discipline very early. A little child has a great capacity to learn and understand. What is "cute" from a two year old can be obnoxious behavior for a four year old. Even a child of a few months can understand "no" and correction or redirection. There is a big difference between acting like a child (what my husband and I used to remind each other was "age-appropriate behavior") and being openly defiant to a parent. Defiance requires immediate discipline. Wrong behaviors require teaching, a redirection to the right way. A young child who is told not to go near the plate of cookies, who waits until your back is turned and snitches one, (while keeping one eye on you to make sure you are not watching her) is being defiant. Not because of the cookie, but because she is openly doing something she was told not to. She requires discipline so she understands who the authority is and that the authority has the power to uphold the rules. God has delegated this responsibility to parents.

On the other hand, a child who comes into the kitchen, knowing the cookies are there for the taking, and begins to climb on the chair to get to the plate and as he does he spills the glass of milk between him and the cookie, is just being a child. This little guy may need to be trained in asking someone else to help him but he should not be punished for the awkwardness of his physical abilities that come with his age.

A very young child needs to gain a working understanding of the hierarchy of authority and how to respect the authorities over him/her.

As a mentor, the authority of the parent needs to be emphasized. If mothers teach their children to understand the authority their parents have over them at a very young age, parenting the rest of their lives will go more easily! Even as they grow and understand the position of other authorities, Sunday School and other teachers, bosses, Pastors, they will function better and be respected in other parts of life. The family is the training ground for the rest of their lives. (A young mother may not understand the authority God has given her as a parent. A look at what the Bible says about the responsibility to raise her children would be very helpful).

At a conference on domestic abuse I heard a couple's testimony that speaks to this issue. Both the husband and wife had been raised in Christian homes. They met at Christian college. They got married and were active leaders in the youth program at their church. At the time I was hearing them they had three children under the age of seven and had been separated for almost two years. After the children were born the husband became abusive, not just verbally but also physically. The final straw for the wife was when he threw her against the wall because she had asked him to take out the trash.

Someone in the audience asked if he had come from an abusive background. He said it was actually the opposite. His parents had a great marriage. He had been blessed with a mother who was able to stay home. He said he does not blame her for his problems, but he can look back and see how she made life easy for him. He didn't have to do anything he didn't want to do. In his marriage, with the addition of each child, his wife asked more and more from him. He had never had such expectations placed on him. He was working hard at trying to resolve the problems now because he had not learned to take responsibility as he was growing up. Before he was married he had not had to sacrifice his own comfort for anyone.

Whoever loves discipline loves knowledge, but he who hates reproof is stupid. Proverbs 12:1

This example, though sad, is good for teaching a young mother of the importance of having expectations and giving responsibility to her children. A wife and 3 children paid the price of an indulgent mother. (I am not taking the responsibility for his own actions off of this man but trying to show that the way parents raise their children is a huge influence on who they are as adults.)

Parents perform an act of love by teaching children to love and worship the Lord, to be responsible and cooperative, to serve, and to show loving-kindness for others. When a mentor sees an indulgent mother or one who is fearful of exerting her authority with her children, please see that teaching her to discipline and have expectations of children is good for them. It is also good for their future spouses and children when they are adults. This teaching will have a generational impact in a family.

The seventh biblical principle to teach is: Parents must be concerned to develop the character of their children. As children grow, they need to acquire character traits pleasing to God. Throughout the Scriptures God has given us examples of obedience by His image bearers that we are to imitate (Philippians 3:17; 2 Thessalonians 3:9; 1 Timothy 1:16). In John 13:15 after He has washed the disciples' feet, Jesus says He has given them (and us) an example that they (and we) should do as He has done.

Romans 5:3-4 tells us suffering produces character and character produces hope. Though disciplining a child may feel like painful suffering, it will result in a lasting hope for parent and child. Hebrews 12:11 points out that, *For the moment all discipline seems painful rather than pleasant, but later it yields the peaceful fruit of righteousness to those who have been trained by it.*

For both the parent and the child, discipline is painful, but in the long-run both are left with great hope for a bright future!

Friends with a large family set a great example to teach young mothers. At the earliest ages of their children they insisted on "first time obedience" on three commands, "No", "Come here," and "Stop." Their children knew the expectation of those commands: they were to drop what they were doing and obey as soon as they heard them. If they did not, they were disciplined for disobedience. Even as adults these children show respect for their parents' authority. All of them are respected in their work places and appear to have good adult relationships with others. Even more importantly, all are followers of Jesus Christ.

Remember, as you mentor a young mother, there are a lot of resources available to help you. Biblical specifics of childrearing are covered in many books and studies available in Christian bookstores and many on-line sources make them readily available.

The last, though perhaps the most important, principle from the Scriptures to teach a young mother is: Her children are a gift from God, entrusted to her and her husband's care.

Behold, children are a heritage from the LORD,
the fruit of the womb a reward. Psalm 127:3

If you were to receive a beautiful family heirloom from your parents as an inheritance, you would treat it as if it were very special. You would want to do whatever you needed to do to preserve it for future generations to use and enjoy. If you took it some place you would pack it in a special container and make sure you knew where it was and who was handling it. You would be particularly careful about to whom you lent it and you would probably have a special place you kept it at home so it would be preserved, not exposed to anything harmful.

Why would we be less diligent with a child? I think back about some places we allowed our children to go, really only learning who the family was and what their character was like by what our children were subjected to in their homes. When we started to study our Bibles, we gave much more thought to the wickedness in the world in seemingly "safe" places. We had based some of our decisions about whose homes our children could visit on the decisions of others we thought were good parents. We later learned they didn't know any more than we did! We were wrong in not fully investigating the situations before granting permission to our own children.

I am grateful for how God spared our children any real harm from being in the homes of other people. If I had it to do over, I would be more careful, especially with overnight stays. Children are precious and are to be treated that way.

If we look at the example set for us in the Scriptures, we find God and Jesus being very kind to, and protective of, their children.

How precious is your steadfast love, O God! The children of mankind take refuge in the shadow of your wings. Psalm 36:7

But Jesus said, "Let the little children come to me and do not hinder them, for to such belongs the kingdom of heaven." Matthew 19:14

When a family follows the biblical prescriptions for raising a family they will have a home providing refuge for their children. Mothers need to be taught the necessity of monitoring what their children watch on TV and movies, many of today's video games are full of violence and sexual content, many are not. Teaching a mother to be vigilant in what she allows as entertainment for her children is helpful, if she has not already thought about it.

A child learns a lot about kindness, humility, and other character traits by how they see their parents live and interact with others. What they see everywhere in the homes of others and in their entertainment choices, also has an effect. Parents need to be aware of the influences their children are introduced to in life. Getting to know the family of a child's friend may help parents be discerning in their decisions about whose house at which their children are permitted to play.

The children who are taught the Word of God, intentionally and by the example set by the way they see their parents live, will be prepared to hear the call of Jesus to come to Him. They cannot be separated from the world, but if a mother understands it is okay to check on what a child is exposed to, her opportunity to be the one to have the major influence increases. What a privilege to offer young mothers encouragement and support to raise their children in the nurture and admonition of the Lord.

Mothering young children is a demanding and, at times, exhausting work. A wonderful attitude for a mentor to adopt when working with a mother of young children is one Paul described in his letter to the Thessalonians. *But we were gentle among you, like a nursing mother taking care of her own children.* 1 Thessalonians 2:7

15
Training In Self Control

...for God gave us a spirit not of fear but of power and love and self-control. 2 Timothy 1:7

Train the younger women to be self-controlled Titus 2:5a

When I was teaching a women's class with a program that provided teaching for the toddlers, I went in to visit the children one morning. The teacher had brought in a crown as an object lesson for the children. After they marched in, sang a song, and had done a little exercise to "get the wiggles out," she opened her Bible and set the crown down in front of her. As she started to tell the story a little boy reached for the crown. She stopped and said he could not touch it yet, when it was time she would pass it around. As she continued to teach, he reached out his right hand for the crown. Just as he was about to touch it, he would lift his left hand, grab his right wrist and jerk it back away from the crown. He waited a minute, never taking his eyes off the crown, then he reached for it again. Just as he got to it, he grabbed his wrist with his other hand and pulled it back. The teacher patiently continued teaching as he did it two or three more times. He never took his eyes off the crown, but he never touched it until she permitted it.

What an act of self-control! He was so tempted to pick it up that he was reaching for it. But he was so determined to obey the rules, he would physically remove the right hand with the left hand. I remember being very impressed at how hard he was working at it!

Food, words, sex, and money, even friends, are all good things. They are to be part of the abundant life God has promised His children when used according to His design. They can also be abused, or misused, in ways not glorifying to God. Teaching a woman who lacks self-control how to apply God's Word to any of these issues will bring her great blessing.

I fear when we talk about the Bible and the command to be self-controlled, most people will automatically think this is not an issue for them because they control their sexual desires and they are   not constantly eating. Pride may keep us from thinking this is an area on which we need to concentrate. But God has given it to us in His list of specific things He wants younger women to be taught. As a centuries old problem, it needs to be addressed. Self-control takes diligence and a desire to please God, even in the little things of life.

By What Standard?

Perhaps our greatest temptation in the area of self-control is to compare ourselves to the world. Eating dinner with friends who are binging (or at least seriously overeating) makes it easy to favorably compare our own eating habits to theirs. When we see a person who is grossly overweight, it is easy to think we are doing fine if we are only a few pounds overweight, even if our eating habits are terrible. Likewise, we hear friends talking about their devotional time and how they don't get to it very often. Suddenly our own devotions done once every couple of weeks look pretty good. Singles who read books and watch movies about singles who are having intercourse or living together before marriage and begin to judge their own standards by the behavior of others can get themselves into trouble.

Our culture encourages us to compare ourselves with others using their behavior as our standard in language use, possessions, worship, child rearing, housekeeping, weight, and finances. As Christians, Jesus and the law of God set our standard for all areas of life.

Do we, as older women wanting to mentor a younger woman, exhibit a level of self-control in those areas of life others need to see modeled? We certainly do not need to be perfect to help another. We should, however, be aware of a lack of self-control so we can point younger women to the truth. The truth is that we are in as desperate a need of the power of the Holy Spirit as she is. Christ is our standard of behavior. He is also our strength to exercise self-control. How do we teach it?

Spiritual Fruit

The Bible has much to say about self-control.

- It is considered a fruit of the spirit
- We are to use it to supplement our faith (2 Peter 1:6).

- We can expect to receive it as something God gives us through His Spirit (2 Timothy 1:6-7).
- It will help us in our marriages (1 Corinthians 7:5).
- It will help us grow in righteousness (James 1:19-20).
- Self-control will help us to continue in faith, love, and holiness (2 Timothy 2:15).

Like all the fruits of the Spirit, as well as all the things we are to teach, an effective tool is to model the fruit we want to see in them.

A man without self-control is like a city broken into and left without walls (Proverbs 25:28). In other words, when we lack self-control, we are subject to attack with no means of defense.

As a fruit of the spirit, we are to exercise self-control in our relationships with other people (Galatians 5:22-23). Proverbs 25:28 says without it life will be unprotected. 2 Timothy 1:7 says we have not been given a spirit of fear, but one of power, love, and self-control. In 2 Peter 1:6, Peter says self-control is something we should add to our knowledge. Knowledge without self-control leads to being ineffective and unfruitful in our knowledge of Jesus Christ (2 Peter 1:9).

Mentoring on the subject of self-control can be very convicting because there are so many areas of life where we must exercise it. Speech (Proverbs 10:9-10), anger (Proverbs 15:18), money (1 Timothy 6:6-10), eating and drinking (Proverbs 23:20), pride (Proverbs 29:23), laziness (Proverbs 20:13), sexual appetites (1 Corinthians 7:5, 9), and our desires in general (James 1:14).

Self-control is an issue in the life of every Christian. The person who gains victory over a temptation to sin one time, sometimes finds herself more vulnerable the next time. A young Christian woman tempted to date an unbeliever may be able to refuse many times but finally be worn down by the pleas or badgering of peers. We hear people talking about a movie or a book, the sex, the violence, or the immorality it displays, and we make an initial decision about it, deciding it would not be a good influence. Then, we hear more and more about it and decide maybe we ought to see for ourselves "just how bad it is." Psalm 119:37 says, *Turn my eyes from looking at worthless things and give me life in your ways.*

There are several ways for a mentor to teach a younger woman self-control. We can give examples of the consequences of a lack of self-control in our own life, we can teach the verses that talk about self-control in the Bible, and we can model it. We also need to remember to continue to pray as we walk through each mentoring relationship. Asking God for clarity in describing the problems we see, His help in what words to use to introduce the subject, and for Him to prepare the heart of our mentee to hear what He wants her to change, will help us help them. We can also remind the women we mentor that they must pray for these attributes when they see the need.

Four areas where the issue of self-control has frequently come up in conversations for me are the areas of housekeeping/use of time, language, passions (including greed, covetousness, money, and things), and food/diet.

1. House Keeping/Use of Time

One of the women who expressed concern about her inability to keep her house clean minimized the problem at first (or I didn't understand). We talked about the "big picture," what needed to be done and how much time she had to do it. Then, she indicated that she couldn't see enough time to do it. She explained I wasn't getting it. Her house was already out of control. Her lack of cleanliness and organization were so bad she was too embarrassed to even let someone come in and help her.

Some problems are not easily overcome. This woman continues to have this struggle. As her children have gotten older she has been able to enlist them in her efforts. She continued to make a clean house a goal she was working on. As she made progress with her commitment to self-control, continuing to clean and organize, she determined not to allow the already cleaned areas to get out of control again. As mentors we can encourage and teach what the bible says, we can offer to help organize and clean, but the plan to accomplish the work and the responsibility for the work belongs to the mentees.

As a gift from God, through the power of the Holy Spirit, self–control needs to be a part of every Christian woman's character traits. If we think of it only in the realm of sin, we will miss a large part of the gift God has to offer us as women, especially as young wives   and mothers just learning to navigate the rivers of marriage and motherhood. Husbands and babies can be so intoxicating, it becomes easy to allow other things to get out of hand. Teaching the discipline of taking care of something while it is still simple to do can bring real peace to a household.

Think of the little things in the home that make life a little nerve wracking. A spill of juice making the whole floor sticky, a room allowed to get out-of-control dirty so cleaning it becomes a major ordeal, or laundry that just does not seem to be done when someone is looking for something.

Stopping what we are doing to clean up juice from the floor as soon as the spill happens, before it is dried and half the household's shoes walk through it, is an act of discipline. Going through the mail every day is easier than waiting until there is a pile a mile high on the counter and there's no workspace left to make dinner. If the clothes would get folded and put away as they come out of the dryer, the laundry never becomes overwhelming. The easy thing to do is to think, "I'll get to it later." In the meantime, things are a mess and a mess affects a family negatively. Orderly is the way God likes things. The people living in order function better than those who live in a mess.

Tackling one area at a time may be a tactic we can advise. If everything in the house is out of control helping a woman to divide the work into bite-sized pieces may help her to get the work organized one room or project at a time rather than having the overwhelming task of getting it all done at once. A mentor might suggest starting with the room most lived in or one project at a time. If part of the problem is too much clothing or too much stuff, she can suggest systematically going through it one room or one kind of item at a time, i.e., go through all the clothes, all the Tupperware, all the toys, whatever is creating the greatest problem or taking up the most usable space.

An added distraction for today's women are social media sites and games galore. The internet seems to be constantly beckoning everyone to come to the computer and waste some time! It is easy for a woman to be pulled into the "social" attraction of these things. It is one of the ways people "connect" today. The question each woman must consider, and perhaps a mentor could ask is, "How much time on-line and playing games is too much time?" Or, "What is not getting done because of the time I spend on these things?" Even as older women we need to consider these questions and set the example of setting our priorities to please God and serve our families. The Lord cares about how we use our time.

Look carefully then how you walk, not as unwise but as wise, making the best use of the time, because the days are evil. Ephesians 5:15-16

We also need to teach that there is no sin in letting something go for a time to accomplish other things. A messy house may be a well lived in house. If it is a lack of self-control causing work to go undone, then there is a problem. If a family has a newborn or a colicky child or even an ill grandparent, if there are other extenuating circumstances, housework may be the thing that gets set aside for a time. I know when my children were small I did not worry about toys lying around or dishes being done until they went to bed. Generally speaking, I could throw all those toys in a bin in a few minutes if I needed to.

Keeping the house for ourselves and our families and using our time wisely are issues most women face daily. It does not seem to matter if we work only at home or also outside the home, the temptation to let housework drop on the list of priorities and the amount of time we waste increase in priority, affects us all.

2. The Use of Words

Language is also an issue that mentors may need to discuss. Especially with a new Christian, some of the language used in our culture is not God-honoring. His name is taken in vain and crude comments are not unusual in many settings.

In my own experience, as a new Christian I used a word with my pastor's wife who very kindly and gently said, "Well, I know what you mean but I would not use that word to describe it." It was a word that had been a normal part of my vocabulary until that point.

The ease with which we fall into using the language of those we spend the most time with is amazing. If foul language is commonplace in an office or school setting, the Christian, unless diligent, may get caught up in it.

I have known a few women who did not even hear themselves when they took the Lord's name in vain. We are so accustomed to hearing it in our day-to-day conversations, and it has become such a habit for so many, our culture is deaf to it. We should not be. Rather than a condemning conversation about how sinful it is, it would be more constructive to have a conversation about how to confess it as the sin it is and stop doing it.

After we have prayed for the Lord to open their ears to the sound of His Name anytime it is used (hopefully every time we use His Name it is not in vain), we may need to suggest they ask for help from someone with whom they spend a lot of time. We might suggest she ask her husband, a roommate, or a co-worker to give her a little sign when she uses a questionable term. Clear the throat, roll the eyes, raise a finger, anything they come up with together, not something obvious to others or condemning, just a reminder to think about the words coming out of her mouth.

A mentor must know what the scriptures say about the words we use and the way we use them. A search for what the Bible says about our words produces a host of wonderful teaching.

Consider these verses as teaching tools:

- *There is one whose rash words are like sword thrusts, but the tongue of the wise brings healing.* Proverbs 12:18
- *Whoever restrains his words has knowledge, and he who has a cool spirit is a man of understanding.* Proverbs 17:27
- *The words of a whisperer are like delicious morsels; they go down into the inner parts of the body.* Proverbs 18:8
- *Do you see a man who is hasty in his words? There is more hope for a fool than for him.* Proverbs 29:20
- *...for by your words you will be justified, and by your words you will be condemned.* Matthew 12:37
- *The good person out of the good treasure of his heart produces good, and the evil person out of his evil treasure produces evil, for out of the abundance of the heart his mouth speaks.* Luke 6:45
- *But now you must put them all away: anger, wrath, malice, slander, and obscene talk from your mouth.* Colossians 3:8

Harsh words, gossip, slander, the Lord's name in vain, and rash words. It may seem like a touchy subject to point out to a young woman that her language does not please the Lord. Pray for the right words to use to approach the subject in love rather than condemnation.

3. Our Passions

Our passions for some things are a powerful influence over us and our ability for self-control. Passions may tempt us in ways God never intended for us to behave. I am thinking of things like money, greed, covetousness, our own comfort, or anything we care so much about that our regular responsibilities are neglected because of it. James says each person is tempted when (s)he is lured and enticed by his (her) own desires (James 1:14). The very next verse says, *Then desire when it has conceived gives birth to sin, and sin when it is fully grown brings forth death.*

Ephesians 4:25-32, though never mentioning self-control, has clear instructions regarding our own understanding:

Therefore, having put away falsehood, let each one of you speak the truth with his neighbor, for we are members one of another. Be angry and do not sin; do not let the sun go down on your anger, and give no opportunity to the devil. Let the thief no longer steal, but rather let him labor, doing honest work with his own hands, so that he may have something to share with anyone in need. Let no corrupting talk come out of your mouths, but only such as is good for building up, as fits the occasion, that it may give grace to those who hear. And do not grieve the Holy Spirit of God, by whom you were sealed for the day of redemption. Let all bitterness and wrath and anger and clamor and slander be put away from you, along with all malice. Be kind to one another, tenderhearted, forgiving one another, as God in Christ forgave you.

These verses do not start by suggesting if a woman has a problem with lying, or anger or stealing, or talking about people, or bitterness, wrath, and clamor, that she should make these things a matter of prayer. They do not suggest she seek counsel about how to deal with them. These verses say if we are caught in the bondage of these things, we should stop. The Scriptures are calling for self-control.

When we are the ones with a passion leading to behavior or an attitude not pleasing to God, we may pray about it (we should pray about it), we may seek wise counsel about how to get out of it, but we also must stop it. We can teach others to do the same. A mentor may have to impress upon a mentee her own responsibility. Though we can offer support and encouragement, she is the one who will need to change her thinking and behavior as we are each responsible for our own. When anyone is convicted of sin, God is calling for obedience.

Rather than praying God would convict us of sin or just make us stop, we need to ask for help, and train those we mentor to ask for His help and understanding. The word "passion" indicates that our feelings about these things are strong. Our comforts, work habits (professional and domestic), sex, anger, money, and the way we handle our relationships are all areas where self-control is necessary. But the grip they hold on our lives is strong. Most people will need help to break that grip.

Show them what the scriptures say. Pray for them to gain victory over the sin. Then, encourage them when they make progress.

4. Food/Diet

In an odd way food and diet are also passions women frequently seem to be fighting. These areas are so big they merit a category all by themselves. I hear this from thin women and from obese women. I personally think about my weight more often than I should. On social media sites I see more and more women turning to exercise in ways that appear to be addictive. Is it possible to be "too self-controlled" about something? Is this obsessive behavior?

The habitual dieter, consumed by her diet and weight, has as big a problem as the grossly obese woman. Food and diet are too big of a deal in her life. Professional help may be needed if her health, and even other parts of her life, become negatively affected. Suggesting professional help needs to come from our desire for her spiritual understanding and growth, not condemnation.

A grossly obese woman once told me God had never convicted her of her sin of overeating. From her words it sounded like she was looking for some kind of guilt feelings so she would know God considered her eating a sin. The Word of God says   gluttony will lead to poverty (Proverbs 23:21). In at least four verses the Scriptures equate gluttons and drunkards. (Deuteronomy 21:20; Proverbs 23:21; Matthew 11:19, and Luke 7:34).

Be not among drunkards or among gluttonous eaters of meat,
for the drunkard and the glutton will come to poverty,
and slumber will clothe them with rags. Proverbs 23:20

The point is, in order for a woman to grow spiritually she needs to come to an understanding of God's warnings in His Word about a behavior or an attitude He calls sin, or what can lead us to sin. We do not need to wait for a "feeling" of guilt to know God wants us to stop a behavior. If His Word prescribes against something, we should stop, just like the instruction to the thief (Ephesians 4:28). When we are doing something and we learn God calls it sin, we should stop it and fall on His mercy, seeking His forgiveness.

There are also women who refuse to eat enough for the body to be well nourished. She too must be challenged with the idol status she has given her physical body. We are to treat it as a temple of the Holy Spirit but not make it a god in and of itself. We care for and preserve our bodies for the service of the Lord. If we are thinking about food and diet or exercise so much that we fail to serve Him, that is a problem that must be addressed.

In a society that honors the perfect body, this may be hard to confront without the Word of God. With the Word of God we can point to the worth of the woman coming from her relationship with the Lord, not her physical perfection. A few verses to consider:

- *For you formed my inward parts; you knitted me together in my mother's womb. I praise you, for I am fearfully and wonderfully made. Wonderful are your works; my soul knows it very well. My frame was not hidden from you, when I was being made in secret, intricately woven in the depths of the earth. Your eyes saw my unformed substance; in your book were written, every one of them, the days that were formed for me, when as yet there was none of them.* Psalm 139:13-16
- *But God, being rich in mercy, because of the great love with which he loved us, even when we were dead in our trespasses, made us alive together with Christ—by grace you have been saved— and*

raised us up with him and seated us with him in the heavenly places in Christ Jesus, so that in the coming ages he might show the immeasurable riches of his grace in kindness toward us in Christ Jesus. For by grace you have been saved through faith. And this is not your own doing; it is the gift of God. Ephesians 2:4-9

- *But God shows his love for us in that while we were still sinners, Christ died for us.* Romans 5:8
- *Let us then with confidence draw near to the throne of grace, that we may receive mercy and find grace to help in time of need.* Hebrews 4:16
- *I have been crucified with Christ. It is no longer I who live, but Christ who lives in me. And the life I now live in the flesh I live by faith in the Son of God, who loved me and gave himself for me.* Galatians 2:20
- *If we confess our sins, he is faithful and just to forgive us our sins and to cleanse us from all unrighteousness.* 1 John 1:9

The area of diet and exercise requiring self-control may need to be emphasized by taking a woman's mind off of them and placing it on how she is serving the Lord and her family, work place, church, etc. It is important to point her to the things that require more of her time and energy and allow the Lord to work in bringing food and diet in line with His plan for her life. The obsession with losing weight may also be an area that requires the attention of a professional counselor.

We all have to eat. We all need exercise. A mother and wife is also responsible to take care of her family with regard to nutrition. Some information and action is a good thing. Food and diet are only a problem when they are the main thing, all the time. Perhaps for the mentor it will be important to look at more than this one portion of the mentee's life. Evaluate if it is too big a deal by what else she is doing. If her family, work, church, and community responsibilities are all in balance, the interest in food may be a new thing or a really healthy habit she has formed.

The Power to Overcome

How do we stop a habit we fight day in and day out, like overeating, too much time on the computer, or foul language? How do we teach someone else to practice self-control? Sometimes habits are so ingrained we aren't even aware of them until the words are already out of our mouths or the food is already in it!

- Pray
- Teach scripture
- Acknowledge and encourage progress
- Set the example

One of the wonderful things God does for each one of His children is to give us the Holy Spirit who dwells in us upon our salvation. He has a very helpful work He does in us and for us.

But the Helper, the Holy Spirit, whom the Father will send in my name,
he will teach you all things and bring to your remembrance all that
I have said to you. John 14:26

...for the Holy Spirit will teach you in that very
hour what you ought to say. Luke 12:12

What a gift!

God, in the person of the Holy Spirit, lives in us and will bring to remembrance all the things we learn from Jesus, who came to fulfill the law not abolish it (Matthew 5:17). Of course, this means we have to give Him something to work with. This is why we want to encourage the women we mentor to study the Word of God, so they will know the words of God when they need them. Exercising self-control is impossible if we do not know what God expects us to do in any particular set of circumstances.

The little boy I talked about in the Toddler class knew that he was to obey his teacher. He had been reminded of that many times. Matthew 6:3 tells us that when we are giving to the poor we should not let our left hand know what our right hand is doing so our giving may be in secret. But in the case of self-control, we can pray that the left hand will help to keep the right hand in line with His commands, just as he was obviously doing for that little boy. We have to teach women to remind themselves of their weaknesses and then practice, practice, practice, just as he did.

The Domino Effect

There are many benefits to learning to be self-controlled, in addition to pleasing God. A woman will see other benefits as she conquers one area where she has lacked self-control. She will see blessings such as lower weight as she controls food, less contention in relationships as she watches her words, a more orderly home as she cleans up and puts things away as needed, etc. She will also see her ability to accomplish the same goal in other areas of life. One at a time, over a period of time, food, the tongue, how we spend money, and getting work done, will all become manageable.

Perhaps one of the important messages we can teach the next generation is that the rewards of exercising self-control are worth the effort required. Some of the rewards that come with this fruit of the spirit:

- Peaceful hearts and homes
- Loving relationships
- Organized living
- Closeness to the Lord

The hardest part of teaching self-control is setting the example!

16
Purity

How can a young man keep his way pure?
By guarding it according to your Word. Psalm 19:9

Train the young women to be pure. Titus 2: 5a

Several years ago my husband and I were invited to attend a professional Lacrosse game in a nearby city. There was a sizable crowd in an indoor arena. Cheerleaders were on the sidelines and vendors roamed throughout the stands. At halftime we were entertained by a show of young girls – I would guess nine and ten years-old – dressed like the cheerleaders in little shorts and tops.

It was heartbreaking. As their mothers stood along the sidelines cheering them on, these young girls spread out over center court and danced a dance you would expect to see in any sleazy dance club. The dance was so provocative and difficult to watch my husband averted his eyes from the dancers. They were just little girls.

If your mother is proudly cheering you on at 9 years old, and your teacher is encouraging this kind of dance before an audience of thousands, what are you learning about purity?

The first definition of "pure" from dictionary.com looks like this: free from anything of a different, inferior, or contaminating kind; free from extraneous matter: *pure gold; pure water.*

This definition is poignant as we think about biblical purity. As a mentor, we want our own lives, as well as the lives of those we mentor, to be free of anything inferior to what God offers. This includes what we put in our minds, how we think, and how we manage money and relationships. Everything we do needs to be handled by principles informed by nothing less than the Word of God. You might think I missed the word "different" in the definition, but the truth of the matter is, if it is different from the Word of God, it is inferior to the Word of God.

As the "older women" or mentors (even as friends), how do we see the biblical expectation of purity? Is it something we know enough about to teach to others?

Purity starts in the heart. It is not just about sexually explicit dancing, cleavage, pre-marital sex, and "R" rated movies, though these are all included. We may encounter women who are confused about purity when they become Christians. Mentoring a woman or leading a small group of women who want to learn about God's design for a woman's purity will require at least these six things from us:

1. An example of scriptural purity
2. The truth from scripture about her purity
3. Honesty
4. Patience
5. Encouragement
6. Prayer

The Scriptural Example and the Scripture

What kind of example do we set for others to imitate? What do we read? What do we watch on TV? Who are our friends? What kind of activities are we involved in? What are our internet habits? Answers to these questions will indicate how pure our own hearts are.

As mentors, the last thing we want to become are the thought and action police. The Holy Spirit is fully capable of convicting a Christian of sin. We do, however, want to teach all areas of thinking and living as important to God and to our own purity. But recognize, we cannot teach anyone more than we have learned, more than what we know to be truth. As with everything we have talked about, it is our own faithfulness to learning the Scripture and setting an example of a pure life that will help us offer the best teaching.

Paul worked at setting this kind of example. In his second letter to the Thessalonians he said, *It was not because we do not have that right, but to give you in ourselves an example to imitate.*

The writer of Hebrews left us with these instructions, *Remember your leaders, those who spoke to you the Word of God. Consider the outcome of their way of life, and imitate their faith.* Hebrews 13:7.

Do we know what the Scriptures say about purity? Some verses to consider and to teach on this topic:

- *Who shall ascend the hill of the LORD? And who shall stand in his holy place? He who has clean hands and a pure heart, who does not lift up his soul to what is false and does not swear deceitfully. He will receive blessing from the LORD and righteousness from the God of his salvation.* Psalm 24:3-5
- *A Psalm of Asaph. Truly God is good to Israel, to those who are pure in heart.* Psalm 73:1
- *How can a young man keep his way pure? By guarding it according to your Word.* Psalm 119:9
- *The thoughts of the wicked are an abomination to the LORD, but gracious words are pure.* Proverbs 15:26
- *The way of the guilty is crooked, but the conduct of the pure is upright.* Proverbs 21:8
- *Blessed are the pure in heart, for they shall see God.* Matthew 5:8
- *Finally, brothers, whatever is true, whatever is honorable, whatever is just, whatever is pure, whatever is lovely, whatever is commendable, if there is any excellence, if there is anything worthy of praise, think about these things.* Philippians 4:8
- *Religion that is pure and undefiled before God, the Father, is this: to visit orphans and widows in their affliction, and to keep oneself unstained from the world.* James 1:27

Looking closely at these verses should help us to see how many aspects of our lives are affected by the presence or absence of purity. Because Psalm 24 tells us the ones who will ascend to God's Holy Hill will be those who are pure, we should want to know, and be willing to talk about, attributes and behaviors exhibiting purity. Psalm 24 says we need *clean hands and a pure heart*. This points out the need for external cleanliness, but if the heart is not pure there is no glory for God in the behavior. Sometimes it is easier to keep the hands from sinning than it is to make the heart happy about doing so!

From these verses other things we could teach would be:

- "Clean hands" come from a pure heart which starts with salvation in Jesus Christ.

- Gracious words reflect a pure heart. We may need to help a mentee rephrase her words or talk about tone of voice if she speaks harshly to her husband or children.
- Purity comes from knowing God's Word. (We always come back to this but it is important in every area of life to know what God says.)
- God gives the desire and the ability to do things according to His Word, to those whose hearts are right with Him. Getting "right" with God starts with repentance and salvation. We may need to teach a woman we are mentoring what these words mean.
- A pure thought life may take work and teaching a woman what pure thoughts are (Philippians 4:8; James 1:27 above). We need to teach that the conviction of the Holy Spirit about our thoughts is not a condemnation from God about who we are, but an invitation from Him to think differently (to be in agreement with Him) and be drawn closer to Him.
- A pure heart will result in good works, visiting orphans and widows, and keeping oneself unstained from the world.

Knowing what to teach and knowing how to teach are different. Purity is a character trait that develops in a woman from the time she is a baby. Upbringing, personal experience, and previous teaching can shape a person's thinking to such a degree that it is hard to replace the thought patterns that have been ingrained in her. Honesty, patience, encouragement and prayer are all tools we can use to help a mentee grow in understanding, faith, and knowledge on the subject of purity (and many others!).

Honesty

We can teach the scriptures all day long. We can encourage women to memorize verses that seem particularly relevant to their needs. But if they do not apply them to their lives, we have given them little help. When we point to the scriptures it may be necessary to (gently) point out where they must be applied.

I recently spoke to a twenty-six year old woman, a relatively new Christian, who had not been raised in a Christian home. Prior to becoming a Christian she wore whatever was trendy. She is large breasted which made the current fashions of low-cut tops very revealing on her. After she began to think about the things of the Lord, a young Christian man told her that a picture he had seen of her on-line was "suggestive." She said she had never thought about her clothing as "saying" anything, or that a shirt or dress could be suggestive of something sexual. She was embarrassed and started to ask other Christians their thoughts on clothing. It was when someone told her that they considered it a sign of respect to other women, as well as to men, to wear clothes that did not attract attention of someone else's husband or boyfriend that she changed the way she dressed.

One young man's honesty about what he saw in a photo led to her conviction about the style of clothes she wanted to wear. She told me that she has decided it is worth the extra time it takes her to shop for the right clothing to communicate respect for others.

That is the kind of honesty we might need to offer a young woman who has not been taught that modest clothes are a part of purity (1 Timothy 2:9).

Clothing is not the only issue that may require honesty in the realm of purity. Speaking harsh words, gossip, or foul language, watching movies or reading books that are not pure in their content, engaging in pre-marital sex or living with a boyfriend, these are all things that need to be honestly and openly discussed. She truly may not know that these affect a woman's purity. Or, she may think "it is not that big a deal," so she does nothing to change things. Until she hears the truth of what God's Word says about her particular set of circumstances, she may not realize that she needs to change.

This kind of honesty is a demonstration of love. We cannot leave someone in their sin before the Lord and say we love them. When we gently approach sin as something that can be changed and, with repentance, God will forgive, we offer a woman hope, peace, and joy.

Patience

"Because I said so" may work with small children but it may take more than that for a grown woman to see the truth of what a mentor presents to her. The young woman who was honestly told about her suggestive picture was embarrassed, but it took a little while longer to completely change her thinking. She read the Bible, she asked other Christians, and she listened for teaching about purity and modesty in the sermons she was hearing. Gradually, as more and more light was shining truth into her thinking, she bought new things, changing the way she dressed to a more modest style.

As mentors, this is why we must be patient and not expect someone to turn their thinking around "because we said so." Allowing a young woman time to be convinced by God makes the change "hers" and not just an outward obedience to something she thinks *we* are commanding. God is patient with us and so we are to be patient with those we mentor.

Several years ago I heard Dr. D.A. Carson speak about his ministry to college students. He had been speaking on college campuses for many years and was seeing big differences in the understanding of the students. Twenty-five years ago he said students came with a basic understanding that there is a God and that he has certain ethical and moral expectations. Now, he said, they no longer have that basic understanding. He has to start with, "There is a God and He cares what you do." He said there are students who make a profession of faith but are horrified when they learn they can no longer live with their boyfriend or have to consider the faith of their boyfriend or girlfriend before they move forward with a relationship.

Patience is required from us while we trust God - as we wait for each woman to make these decisions about her own purity. While we wait we can continue to teach them what God's Word says, be honest about where it needs to be applied to their lives, encourage them as we see progress, and pray. These are the things that will shine the light of truth on the life of a believer.

Encouragement
Therefore encourage one another and build one another up, just as you are doing .1 Thessalonians 5:11

As we speak truth and patiently wait for a woman to begin to do things a new way, God's way, we may also need to encourage her as she deals with difficult decisions. Moving out from living with a boyfriend may not be financially feasible on a moment's notice.

Completely replacing a music or movie collection may take her going through them one more time, "just to make sure they really need to go." Buying a new wardrobe may require time to accumulate the money to do it. It may even take sitting through a movie and experiencing the conviction of the Holy Spirit for a woman to be completely convinced that she needs to make a change in her habits to become more pure before God.

When a mentor acknowledges the reality of these delays and builds a mentee up for each positive step she makes, she is encouraging her to continue to grow in knowledge and understanding of God. Encouragement gives the mentee confidence to keep trying, to take the next step toward making things right. Some of us have been Christians for so long that we have forgotten how long it took us (or others) to fully understand (are we there yet?) and implement what God calls us to do. This is especially true if one has been living apart from the Lord as an adult. Hopefully, our encouragement will speed up the process!

Especially with a new believer, encouragement may be reinforcing what we have taught. If a woman tells us she was "so uncomfortable" with her friends who were drinking and talking about things she used to be interested in but no longer enjoys, we may need to point out to her that this is probably the conviction of the Holy Spirit. To explain to her that the feeling of being uncomfortable is the work of the Holy Spirit growing her faith encourages her that God is at work in her!

Encouragement can be offered in many ways:

- Congratulate her on getting out of an unhealthy relationship.
- Notice and compliment a new modest outfit.
- Suggest books and movies that will entertain without causing her to sin.
- Point out when God appears to be offering new friends or new ways of thinking.
- Affirm every effort at doing something God's way

Ask God and He will provide even more words and opportunities to offer encouragement because we are looking for them.

Prayer

The necessity for prayer is obvious. We need prayer so we can ask where to start and what the Lord would have us teach from His Word. We need prayer so we will be honest, patient, and encouraging. The women we work with need to be prayed for so they will understand what purity is to God, according to his Word, and how to apply what they learn to their lives.

Woe to you, scribes and Pharisees, hypocrites! For you clean the outside of the cup and the plate, but inside they are full of greed and self-indulgence. You blind Pharisee! First clean the inside of the cup and the plate, that the outside also may be clean. Matthew 23:25-26

Every woman we mentor will come with different thoughts, teachings, and expectations about what purity is and how she is to live it out. If a woman with a true desire from God comes to you or me wanting to learn to live His way with regard to purity, it probably means she has seen something that tells her we know what to teach her. Sometimes it is easy for others to look at us and see that the outside of the cup is clean and so they want to know what we know. You and I know that the outside of the cup is not the whole story for any one of us. What is on the inside of the cup is important before God and it is where we will teach from.

Will you examine your thoughts? Will you pay attention to the choices you are making with regard to entertainment, books and movies? Will you listen to your own speech and ask God to show you if it is not pure?

Sexual purity, purity of thoughts, purity of words, and purity in our conduct, all flow from what is in our hearts. Though none of us will set the perfect example of purity in this life, do we know enough about it and practice it enough to set an example and teach it?

17
Busy at Home

She looks well to the ways of her household and does not eat the bread of idleness. Proverbs 31:27

I am the fifth of six children. My mother stayed home with us for many years, not going into the workplace until my youngest brother was in the third grade. I can remember the summer before he entered the first grade (no kindergarten for our family) many people would hear he was going to school and ask her, "What will you do with all your time once they are all in school?" She was horrified every time. She had a lot to do to keep up with a husband, six children, a house, a yard, PTA, and church responsibilities. She could not imagine ever having time to do nothing.

When she did go back to work it was because college was in sight for the oldest and my parents wanted to help us financially if we wanted to seek higher education.

The Feminist Influence

Though my own Mother was at home for many years, I am a product of the mentality of the early 1970's. In my teenage years I was bombarded by the feminist movement. It was everywhere. I was taught a woman could only be fulfilled by getting a college degree and embarking on a successful career. It was the only way to maximize her full potential. Some of my peers believed having children was an obstacle to achieving any real goals. I will never forget the poster in a woman's dorm on my college campus. It was a picture of a fish riding a bicycle. Underneath it said, "A woman needs a man like a fish needs a bicycle." Such was the world's thinking of the day.

My own mother loved family and wanted us to be married and have children, but she also wanted her children to have college educations. She taught me that, as a woman, I needed to be prepared, "What if you get married but he dies, or leaves, or is injured and can't work? You need to be able to take care of yourself." She was so convincing that all four of her daughters have college educations. (I am sincerely grateful for her encouragement regarding education and do not mean to imply that a woman should not go to college.)

I think it's interesting to note the feminist movement did not just convince women we needed to be "more than a wife and mother," men were also retrained to believe it was what every woman wanted. "A woman's place is in the home," became a highly criticized way of thinking.

During these years when feminism was prevalent, if someone, man or woman did not believe it was better for the woman to have a career outside of home, they were taken in by, "Two incomes are needed to run a household today." Many of my peers had husbands who wanted them to work outside of the home because they wanted the lifestyle and financial freedom a second income could provide.

Just for the record, I know there are families who could not make ends meet without a second income. Whether it needs to be a second job for Dad or a job for Mom (many of which can be from home) is a decision each family needs to make. There are also many families who, from appearances, have survived with relationships intact with the wife/mother in the workplace. I felt like I had the best of both worlds, home and work, when I worked part-time outside the home when my children were young

Though I was taught to think of myself first and work hard to get a good job, I found that my Christianity challenged my thinking after about fifteen years of marriage. When I learned I was created as a helpmate for my husband, I was stunned. I never thought that meant I could not work, but I was clearly taught that the Bible expects me to actually be his helper, and to be more concerned about home than work. The biblical priority list for a wife and mother would be God (Exodus 20:3), husband (Genesis 2:18, 24), children, and then work and ministry outside the home. As the scriptures challenged me, so a mentor should allow it to be a challenge to your mentee's thinking as well. When we point a young woman to the scriptures, God, through His Holy Spirit and His Word, will make the changes He desires. Regardless of our own understanding or family decisions, we must point a mentee to the Word of God.

It is important to understand God's teaching regarding a woman's role as wife and mother. We can, again, start with the Proverbs 31 woman.

All About Home
As we read Proverbs 31:10-31 we can see the Proverbs 31 woman was very busy. Not all of her business was "in" the home but it was all "about" the home. For many, she is more than a little intimidating as an example!

31.10   An excellent wife who can find? She is far more precious than jewels.

31.11   The heart of her husband trusts in her, and he will have no lack of gain.

31.12   She does him good, and not harm, all the days of her life.

31.13   She seeks wool and flax, and works with willing hands.

31.14   She is like the ships of the merchant; she brings her food from afar.

31.15   She rises while it is yet night and provides food for her household and portions for her maidens.

31.16   She considers a field and buys it; with the fruit of her hands she plants a vineyard.

31.17   She dresses herself with strength and makes her arms strong.

31.18   She perceives that her merchandise is profitable. Her lamp does not go out at night.

31.19   She puts her hands to the distaff, and her hands hold the spindle.

31.20   She opens her hand to the poor and reaches out her hands to the needy.

31.21   She is not afraid of snow for her household, for all her household are clothed in scarlet.

31.22   She makes bed coverings for herself; her clothing is fine linen and purple.

31.23   Her husband is known in the gates when he sits among the elders of the land.

31.24   She makes linen garments and sells them; she delivers sashes to the merchant.

31.25 Strength and dignity are her clothing, and she laughs at the time to come.

31.26 She opens her mouth with wisdom, and the teaching of kindness is on her tongue.

31.27 She looks well to the ways of her household and does not eat the bread of idleness.

31.28 Her children rise up and call her blessed; her husband also, and he praises her:

31.29 "Many women have done excellently, but you surpass them all."

31.30 Charm is deceitful, and beauty is vain, but a woman who fears the LORD is to be praised.

31.31 Give her of the fruit of her hands, and let her works praise her in the gates.

This woman works hard! She works late and rises early to cook for her household. She is productive at home but she also "considers a field and buys it" and "plants a vineyard." Well-known Christian commentator Matthew Henry suggests, "with the fruit of her hands" may mean from the profits of her handmade (I would point out home-made) goods (Proverbs 31:24) she is able to pay to plant the vineyard. She makes fabrics and then clothing and she "brings her food from afar." In other words, she goes where she needs to go to get what her family needs. Verse 27 seems to sum it all up like this; *She looks well to the ways of her household and does not eat the bread of idleness.*

Her example leaves me in a pile of guilt some days. The children of that virtuous Proverbs 31 woman are not naked because she supplies the linen for their clothing. Well-dressed children and a diligent wife make her and her home blessed. Her husband finds honor at the gate (where he conducts his business) partly because she is a helper with strength and dignity. He benefits by her accomplishments and reputation.

In comparison, my life is easy. As long as my husband and I have work, we have money, and I can just run to the mall. No weaving or sewing required, saving me many hours to keep my children well-dressed!

If I spend my whole day (or many in a row) wasting time, watching videos, playing around on the internet, gossiping   with girlfriends, or shopping for things I don't need (for the record, I try really hard not to waste time like that!), I can still throw a beautiful meal together in the last half-hour before my husband gets home. I can buy it pre-cooked, pre-packaged, or prepared for me! Any Mom could also do this when she spends a serious day homeschooling her children or running them from one event or practice to another. Or, like the Proverbs 31 woman, if we used our time reaching out to the poor or doing some other kind of work, we can get a healthy meal on the table without spending hours in the kitchen. I am thankful for these modern conveniences.

It seems the Proverbs 31 woman was able to do it all, work at home, work outside as was necessary, and minister to others. She did it all but the important virtue for her was that she feared the Lord. Love for Him was the reason she did all she did.

As mentors, we must examine to see if our own lives set the same example of one who fears the Lord. Whether we work outside the home, stay at home and run the household full time, or do some combination of working outside and inside the home, it is necessary to do it to the glory and honor of God. American women have a lot of freedom because of what conveniences are available to us in our day. As a mentor we have a lot of responsibility to set the right example and teach the next generation how to use the resources and freedom God has given us for His glory, and the good of our families.

The question is, how do we teach others the answer to this question, "What's right for a Mother to do?" Does she work outside the home? Stay at home? Work from home? Homeschool the children? Volunteer in the school the family chooses outside of home? We live in a world of choices.

As we have seen before, according to Deuteronomy 6:6-9, it is important for parents to understand that they have the primary responsibility for teaching their children.

Every Christian family has to make a decision about how the children will be educated, academically and spiritually. Whether or not we believe it, both academics and religion are taught in every school setting. God holds parents responsible for the teaching of the children in both academic and spiritual realms (Deuteronomy 6:7 and Psalm 78:4,5).

Public schools have many risks to them, the teaching is not just lacking God, in many cases, it is anti-God. Christian schools are expensive and homeschooling is labor intensive. Before God, parents need to make a unified decision about educating children.

As mentors we can talk about this decision. We can help a young woman investigate the options in her own town and we can pray with her about the education of her children. Ultimately, she and her husband have to make the decision. If we don't agree we can say so. Whether we agree or not, we can then do all we can to support these parents' responsibility to know what is happening in the lives of their children, whatever they have chosen. There is no form of education where children are not at risk of being introduced to things that parents need to know about in order to correct. Even homeschooled children are exposed to worldly thinking and may have even more access to dangerous internet sites than a child who attends a school outside the home.

Interestingly, the Bible in Deuteronomy and Proverbs gives the father the primary responsibility for teaching the children, but mothers are not left out. Proverbs 1:8-9 say, *Hear, my son, your father's instruction, and forsake not your mother's teaching, for they are a graceful garland for your head and pendants for your neck.* This reference to both parents teaching is repeated in Proverbs 6:20. Women need to be encouraged that they are to have an active role in the education of their children. If they are homeschooled, she may be the primary teacher. If they are in any other school setting, both parents will have to be aware of, and involved in, the learning process. Even if a woman is home-schooling, the stay-at-home Mom these days does not "stay at home." Most families have two cars. Most children, whether they are homeschoolers, in Christian school, or public school, are involved in activities outside the home. Most Moms are free to come and go from home to be involved, and to involve their children, in things outside of the house.

Like the Proverbs 31 woman, almost all of us bring our food from afar (though personal gardening is making a comeback as the price of groceries increases). We rarely weave the fabric but we all choose it at a store (unless we order it off the internet!). We are still responsible to see that our families have clothing, eat well and learn the basics of health and nutrition. It is a big responsibility. It may be useful to a young woman to help her examine what her strengths and weaknesses are as a wife and mother. Then, you and she can seek ways to help her where she needs it.

When I homeschooled my own children, which I did for just three years, my son and I battled almost every day for several months (more about this in Chapter 17). He did not think I was the best teacher and I certainly did not like his lack of cooperation. It did not get better until I told our homeschool evaluator, a woman who works with children, about this. She gave me sound advice that I will explain more about later.

It required hearing the truth of my own mistakes to bring about change. It was a gift, one I think many mentors can give if they are willing to speak the truth so those they are working with can see what they need to change.

The Long Term View

As a mentor, perhaps one of the more important things we can do for the young mother is to give her an understanding of the long term view. We do not want to point her to just what is good for her immediate set of circumstances within the family, but to teach her to look for how the consequences of any decision she makes today, will affect her children and grandchildren and their children and grandchildren. Every parent carries this generational responsibility into every decision. Christian families can be so affected by our Western culture that they are more concerned for the things of the world (a bigger house or more things) than the things of God (the spiritual training of our children). God is future-oriented, not things-oriented, and we should be, too.

The long term view of being "busy at home" will help parents make decisions about what it will look like now for the benefit of those who will receive instruction, leading to the fear and admonition of the Lord later. We are responsible to teach and set an example of following God's Word and His commands as the basis for the decisions we make about everyday life. Our goal is the glory of God and the good of the next generation. If a daughter or young woman learns this, she will be equipped to make decisions with her husband according to God's Word.

The feminist movement has left a remarkable imprint on our culture. Sadly, in my experience, many Christians have not been taught the full truth of God's Word about parents' responsibilities to teach the children God entrusts to them, as well as providing for them and protecting them. Though there are many families today who are victims of a bad economy and require a second income just to make ends meet, there are also some Christians who are looking for worldly approval and gain. If a young woman comes to a mentor saying she wants to be at home with her children rather than in the workplace, it would be helpful to look with her at the financial decisions and values that have her there. Perhaps she can incrementally go from full-time to part-time and eventually to work from home. It may take an objective set of eyes to help her see what she needs to do.

Obviously, a single mother has to do the best she can do to support her children. A lot of prayer needs to go into the decisions she makes about childcare and education. A mentor to support and encourage her as she does would be a great gift for her. The mentor will need to be the flexible one as a single mother does not usually have ready access to childcare or extra money to meet at a restaurant or coffee shop. She will be busy at home when she is there because no one shares the responsibility. Regardless of how she got there, her overall responsibility is complicated and stressful. If she loves the Lord, she will want to raise her children to love Him, too.

The model of the Proverbs 31 woman teaches that managing the home is the work of the woman. She is not expected to be in it alone. She is responsible to be a part of decision-making discussions with her husband about who and how these responsibilities will get covered in the family. One goal seems to be the peace and comfort of the family and the home. She shares the responsibility to raise the children in the fear and admonition of the Lord and is to be her husband's helpmate in this. This is done in a warm and welcoming home where hospitality is offered to others. She may make money, perhaps she will spend hours away from home to do it, but her priority is to be with her family and the home she makes for them.

Here are a few of the questions that have arisen regarding the woman who is "busy at home":

1. Can she earn money? Yes, Proverbs 31:16 *She considers a field and buys it; with the fruit of her hands she plants a vineyard.* Proverbs 31:24 *She makes linen garments and sells them; she delivers sashes to the merchant.*
2. Can she be involved in ministry? Yes, Proverbs 31:20 *She opens her hand to the poor and reaches out her hands to the needy.*
3. Can she influence others outside of her household? Yes, Proverbs 31:26 *She opens her mouth with wisdom, and the teaching of kindness is on her tongue.*
4. Can she influence her city, her town, etc. and receive recognition for what she does? Yes, Proverbs 31:31 *Give her of the fruit of her hands, and let her works praise her in the gates.*
5. Can she use her gifts and talents? Yes, Proverbs 31:25 *Strength and dignity are her clothing, and she laughs at the time to come.* Proverbs 31:26 *She opens her mouth with wisdom, and the teaching of kindness is on her tongue.*

As we look at these questions and answers we cannot lose sight of Proverbs 31:30: *She is a woman who fears the Lord.* The implication is she does what pleases the Lord. I think this can be accomplished by a woman who prays and sets her priorities according to God's Word.

Developing Talents And Gifts

In many ways the woman who chooses to be busy at home full time is more likely to develop her own talents and gifts without waiting for the "empty nest" when she will have a lot more 'free' time. If she is organized and resourceful so her family is well cared for, she should have time to use her gifts for her own and her family's benefit. She is not bound by a work schedule, allowing her to develop her own skills outside of those her work demands. If we can teach and pass on the long-term view of generational responsibility, she will recognize the amount of influence her own example will set and be able to teach the next generation.

Intentional Influence

Regardless of the current situation a woman finds herself in, we can try to teach younger women the priority of God, husband, and children so the subsequent generations are raised to serve and love the Lord. If a married woman's home is her priority because she has a healthy fear of the Lord, Proverbs 31 teaches us that it will benefit her husband and their children. Her efforts will be blessed.

Only take care, and keep your soul diligently, lest you forget the things that your eyes have seen, and lest they depart from your heart all the days of your life. Make them known to your children and your children's children.

Deuteronomy 4:9

18
Training In Kindness

Train the younger women to be kind. Titus 2:5d

A man who is kind benefits himself, but a cruel man hurts himself.
Proverbs 11:17

"Be nice!" "Say you're sorry." "Watch your tone of voice." "Be more careful how you say things." "Everyone is good at something." "How would you like it if she did that to you?" "Do unto others as you would have them do unto you." "Don't tattle!" "And, what did you do to her?"

My mother did not teach us to memorize Bible verses, but when I think back she taught us a lot about being kind. I can still hear her voice as she gave us these admonitions again and again.

Sadly, the most predominant place for *un*kindness is in the home! I was an adult probation/parole officer before I was married. I remember being surprised by the statistic that 85% of all murders were crimes of passion, committed by someone the victim was close to. Predictable, I guess. Our loved ones are the people who know us well enough to get so angry they want to kill us.

The sin nature in a person can lead anyone into some pretty awful sin against others. The closer our relationship with someone, the more likely we know enough about him/her to either anger or delight us.

We are also capable of being kind to them, with the help of the Holy Spirit. As a mother or a wife we can use kind words rather than harsh or critical words to encourage cooperation or understanding.

I started to homeschool our son when he was in the fifth grade. Raising my voice and taking privileges seemed a natural response when he refused to do his work. My anger would then ratchet the argument up notch by notch. Nothing was accomplished. As I mentioned before, our evaluator (required in the state of Pennsylvania) offered the solution to this problem. When I became angry, and signaled it by raising my voice, she pointed out that my son then considered the problem mine. I had a problem, and he was happy to let me deal with it. What I was trying to convey was that my son had work to do, not me! Obviously, I needed a better approach!

In an act of discipline and the power of the Holy Spirit, I changed my responses because of her instruction. I never (okay, almost never!) raised my voice again, but gave him a matter-of-fact "to do" list and a clear understanding of the consequences for work not done. These instructions were usually written, but if spoken, I tried to use a respectful tone of voice and kind words. He started doing his work! I got completed work. He got the benefit of learning, and his privileges were reinstated. A win-win situation! Kindness and respect had won over anger and arguing.

"Be Nice" Culture

In any mentoring situation we have to convey the truth that the Bible is clear that it is God who gives us the ability, with the power of the Holy Spirit, to be kind. God is kind and we are to follow His example. Unfortunately, the world has redefined "kind." From an eternal perspective it is unkind of us to leave a person in her sin so she misses the opportunity to repent and believe Christ has taken the punishment for it. Without this knowledge and commitment, any person is condemned to an eternity in Hell.

The new, worldly definition of kindness includes not telling someone she is wrong or in sin. Correcting someone else's child when we are in a position of authority over them is even considered unkind or wrong. Even disciplining our own children isn't acceptable to some in our "be nice" culture.

Such thinking is surrender; surrender to the promptings of the tempter or surrender to our own lazy impulses. Thinking we never have to confront someone with sin, or we can allow a friend to remain in sin and back it up with Scripture, "who am I to cast the first stone?" is an easier way to live.

But it does not line up with the whole counsel of God. Romans 2:4 says, *Or do you presume on the riches of his kindness and forbearance and patience, not knowing that God's kindness is meant to lead you to repentance?* The kindest thing we can do for another person is point her to her need for a Savior, so she will see the need for repentance.

As mentors and believers in Jesus Christ, it is important to show kindness because it is obedient to God and it brings Him glory, not to mention it really improves our relationships with others! When we teach other women to show kindness it is important to teach biblical kindness, including telling the truth in love, with gentleness (Ephesians 4:15, 4:1-2).

This is something I like to define at a first meeting with a new mentee. I do not want her to be surprised when I point out that something she has told me is sin. If she knows going in that I am seeking to bring her into a restored and growing relationship with the Lord and the people she loves, she is more likely to receive correction well.

Keep this in mind: being nice is not necessarily kind. When we nicely decide not to tell a woman that her actions are sinful, we are leaving her in that sin and in conflict with God and His Word. That is not kind.

So, what does the Bible say about kindness? There are twenty eight verses in the Bible that mention the word. They will give us biblical examples of what it means to show kindness.

The word is first used in Genesis 19:19 regarding Lot and God's kindness shown to him in providing him a warning to get out of the city before He destroyed it. Genesis 19:17-19 say, *And as they* (the two angels sent by God) *brought them out, one said, "Escape for your life. Do not look back or stop anywhere in the valley. Escape to the hills, lest you be swept away." And Lot said to them, "Oh, no, my lords. Behold, your servant has found favor in your sight, and you have shown me great kindness in saving my life. But I cannot escape to the hills, lest the disaster overtake me and I die."*

Saving a life is certainly a kind act! Giving the warnings of the things which are not pleasing to God ("Do not look back or stop") is also showing kindness.

The second time the word is used, Abraham expects his wife, and Sarah agrees, to show kindness to him by asking her to say she is his sister rather than his wife (Genesis 20:13). When asked why he sought such an agreement, Abraham said, *I did it because I thought, "There is no fear of God at all in this place, and they will kill me because of my wife. Besides, she is indeed my sister, the daughter of my father though not the daughter of my mother, and she became my wife. And when God caused me to wander from my father's house, I said to her, 'This is the kindness you must do me: at every place to which we come, say of me, He is my brother'"* (Genesis 20:11 – 13).

Abraham justifies this half-truth as a matter of protection. Sarah kindly concedes the point and God ratifies their decision by blessing Abraham and protecting both Sarah and Abraham from harm.

There are several times Paul mentions kindness in his letters to believers where he gives us some good explanations of what kindness should look like. In 1 Corinthians 13:4 Paul is instructing us how to love. He starts with patience and kindness (gifts of the spirit), but continues to describe them, giving us some of their attributes. Verses 4 – 6 say, *Love is patient and kind; love does not envy or boast; it is not arrogant or rude. It does not insist on its own way; it is not irritable or resentful; it does not rejoice at wrongdoing, but rejoices with the truth.*

When we look closely at that list, these are kind ways of showing love. There is no kindness, ever, in envy, boasting, arrogance, rudeness, insisting on our own way, being irritable or resentful, or rejoicing in wrongdoing. Paul's description includes things we do when we are not showing kindness to those we love. He is encouraging us to show love by being patient and kind, which include being generous, humble, polite, considerate of other's desires, cheerful, grateful, and rejoicing in what is right.

In Ephesians 4:32 Paul goes on to include forgiving in his definition of kindness. He says, *Be kind to one another, tenderhearted, forgiving one another, as God in Christ forgave you.* And in Philippians 4:14 he says we are kind when we share the troubles of another, *Yet it was kind of you to share my trouble.*

There is also just good old compassionate kindness when we recognize a need and fill it. In Acts 28 Paul is on a ship bound for Rome where he is to be tried by Caesar with no clear charges against him (Acts 25:27). On the way to Rome the ship is wrecked during a storm. For fourteen days the sailors were "violently storm tossed," (27:18), without food for many days (27:21), and afraid of how it might end (27:29-30). They ran aground on the Island of Malta. In Acts 28:2 Paul describes the kindness shown to them by the people of

Malta, *The native people showed us unusual kindness, for they kindled a fire and welcomed us all, because it had begun to rain and was cold.* These natives saw the need of those storm-tossed men and built a fire to warm them from the cold. Later he says they showed hospitality to them for three days.

These examples in the Scripture show us kindness is multi-faceted. We can show kindness in words and in deeds. We can be kind in a momentary act or show kindness in hospitality for days at a time. We are also reminded how God has shown kindness to us.

Speaking Truth

Generally, women want to be kind. It is a part of the nurturing nature women are given by God. But, there are certain people in our lives to whom it is difficult to be kind. Some people make it hard. So why bother? If we are usually kind, is it okay to be unkind to someone who is too hard for us?

This is another area others will benefit from understanding the blessing of obedience, an important principle to teach. God's word tells us there will be rewards for us in this life when we are kind. I don't think this necessarily means we should invite a person over for Sunday dinner who has an unrepented history of unkindness toward us. There are many ways to show kindness without having a close friendship with someone. We set an example when we acknowledge them when we see them, listen when they speak in a more public setting, and point them to the Lord if we must interact with them in some way.

Look at the rewards promised by God for kindness.

- *A man who is kind benefits himself, but a cruel man hurts himself.* Proverbs 11:17
- *Whoever pursues righteousness and kindness will find life, righteousness, and honor.* Proverbs 21:21
- *But the fruit of the Spirit is love, joy, peace, patience, kindness, goodness, faithfulness, gentleness and self-control.* Galatians 5:22-23a

Teaching another to demonstrate kindness to other people is to her advantage, especially if she is meeting their needs, because God will bless her for the effort. There are people who might say we should not do something just for the reward, but out of love for God and gratitude for what He has done for us we obey Him. I agree. But when He offers us a benefit, why not enjoy it? If the reward is God's blessing, I want it! We need to teach others that God's blessings are so good that they should want them, too. I think it is important to point out it is part of what makes us love Him so much. He is kind to us when we are kind to others!

When God is kind to us it is for our good, we benefit. In Hosea 11:4 God speaks of how He treated Israel, *I led them with cords of kindness, with the bands of love, and I became to them as one who eases the yoke on their jaws, and I bent down to them and fed them.* In his letter to the Ephesians Paul points out that it is because of God's rich mercy and great love for us that he promises them, *that in the coming ages he might show the immeasurable riches of his grace in kindness toward us in Christ Jesus (*Ephesians 2:5,7*).*

When we show kindness, we are imitating Christ. When we are willing to teach other women to do the same thing, they too, will be imitating Christ. They will be headed for quite a blessing.

As we mentor another woman, it is our responsibility, and God-given opportunity, to speak the truth she needs to hear. We should try to be as gentle and kind as possible, even though we may not sound kind in the moment.

In a mentoring situation a young woman may describe an argument with her husband where he uses disrespectful words or unkind accusations toward her. In her response she unloads her own critical attack on him. Pointing out her sin is our responsibility and God-given opportunity. Neither she nor we can change her husband's approach, but as a child of the Lord, she has the power of the Holy Spirit to respond without retaliating. She needs to hear she was wrong in her response, even though she had also been wronged. God wants us to put away all anger (Colossians 3:8). This may be a hard truth for her to hear but leaving her with the impression we approve of her response does not grow her understanding of God's plan or commands for her marriage (or any relationship if she is responding in anger).

In The Little Things

Sadly, there are plenty of people in the world who, from a young age, saw little or no kindness modeled for them. The Bible's command to always consider others more significant than ourselves does not come naturally for anyone. It is even harder for those who did not ever see it modeled. I have heard professional counselors say, "Wounded people wound people." Because of this, and because kindness is an attribute which it is hard to teach someone, we must be kind when we mentor. Perhaps, our willingness to mentor is an act of kindness in and of itself. It is. Kindness, though, can be (and probably should be) more spontaneous.

One May our property was hit by a hail storm with golf-ball sized stones. Our yard was a wreck. Leaves and branches down, flowers torn apart, and so many pinecones! I raked them into about twenty-five piles so it would be manageable. Our neighbors told us we could take the debris behind their house and compost it with theirs. My first trip was difficult as I am not used to wheelbarrows. Dropping it off the curb onto the street was tricky as I tried to balance the load and not lose it.

My husband was also working with me. When I came back with the second load to cross the street he had taken some bricks and built me a small ramp. The wheelbarrow rolled right down them without my losing the load! I was thrilled. It was a small but very helpful kindness. Quite frankly, it did not occur to me that there was a solution to my problem. That simple ramp, that simple encouragement, kept me going.

This is the kind of "as we go" kindnesses that can encourage a young mother or wife as she is moving through life trying to do the next right thing in her marriage. As a mentor, with kindness on our lips, with love for her in our hearts, and a desire to encourage, we can model kindness in the moment.

There are many ways to do this. Speaking truth is one of them. We can also actively listen to what is happening in her life and respond with kindness and compassion. If she is anticipating a busy time, can we accommodate her schedule or take the children for a few hours? Would it be better for her if we met early in the morning or in the evening, at her house or our house? Would an occasional meal be helpful to her?

Kindness is active, never finished, and constantly a command for the child of God. We all love it when others are kind to us. In our mentoring relationships, one way both people can benefit is by following Luke's directive from Luke 6:3, *And as you wish that others would do to you, do so to them.*

19
The "S" Word...Submission

Train the young women...to be submissive to their own husbands.
Titus 2:5b

I was not a Christian when I got married and this "submission" concept, actually just the sound of the word, made my skin crawl and my blood boil! In my mind only weak women needed their husbands to "run the show." I certainly never wanted anyone to think of me as weak or not in complete control. My poor husband!

Once I came to know the Lord and He gave me a real desire to know His Word, this doctrine seemed to be everywhere I looked. I could not get away from the idea. I could not find any place in Scripture taking me off the hook to obey it. What I did find was what a gentle, loving, protective doctrine it is.

As far back as Joseph, Moses, and David, when the people of God submitted to the will of God (as opposed to all the times they chose to go their own way), life was better. God only asked them to do what He knew would be better for them and His people. Our Heavenly Father always gives instructions, not just for His glory, but for our good. This truth took me a long time to incorporate into my thinking. It is an essential truth to teach younger women. When we do things His way, we are the ones who benefit. Young women need to be taught that the command to submit to our husbands' authority is a good thing when understood properly. Obeying God brings blessings to every woman (and her family) trusting God by living as He calls us to in our marriages.

The Hammer And The Nail
The questions arise about submission because of a lack of understanding of what God is asking for, from both men and women. In order to teach the next generation and younger women the truth of God's goodness in this instruction to submit, we must understand it ourselves.

In the discussion of submission, some people miss two important verses. The first tells Christians that we are to submit to one another. The second tells men they are to love their wives as Christ loves the church. Ephesians 5 goes on to point out Christ laid down His life for the church. A man, if thinking and living biblically, actually has the much more difficult part of the marriage relationship! Unfortunately, men who do not think and live biblically give submission a bad reputation.

In *The Way Home,* Mary Pride wrote that she had always thought of submission as the relationship of the hammer and the nail. "The husband got to be the hammer and the poor wife was the nail." She goes on to say, "I hadn't seen that the issue is not power and force, but structure and roles."[7]

As she continues to look at what happened to our original roles in marriage she observes, "In the beginning God created marriage with a division of labor and responsibility. Man was to subdue the earth, and woman was to help him, and together they were supposed to be fruitful and multiply." She then makes a great case for how feminism and careerism confuse those roles. Today, there is no clear, cultural understanding of how men and women are to keep a biblical marriage together doing what God has commanded. This is not to say that the Bible does not address it.

Over the years I tried it all. I worked full time until my children were born. After they were born I worked part-time, as many as thirty hours a week at one point and as few as ten hours a week at another point. I was constantly thinking I needed to "keep my foot in the door." The truth is our marriage was never better than those times when I worked outside the home little, or not at all. I look back and realize it is because those are the ideal circumstances for a mother of young children who wants to keep her home, her husband, and her children thriving. There is much less stress on Momma when she can take care of her primary responsibilities without having her loyalties divided by work obligations or responsibilities.

---

[7] Pride, Mary, *The Way Home,* Home Life Books, Fenton, MO, 1985, page 196

When a woman needs to work in order to help keep a roof over the heads of the family and food on the table, part of the divided loyalty will be between work (employer) and husband. Something has to give and the children, especially if they are young, will require attention. Dad is usually the one who gets neglected. This is a statement of fact, not a judgment on the woman who works outside the home. She may need to be more intentional in her marriage relationship and her husband may need to understand the pressures on his wife. Communication between them will be critical.

Work or no work, we are called to submit. The helpful definition finally given to me in my rebellious years, was "voluntary agreement." I could live with that. Voluntarily agreeing with my husband was somehow easier than submitting to him. When we submit to one another we are working together for the good of our marriage and family. There always needs to be compromise. Both spouses should feel free enough in the love and respect of his/her spouse to be the one to compromise in any decision. Submission is a choice.

Respectfully Submitted

I am a woman with strong opinions. Somewhere along my Christian way I received advice saying a woman is to speak her mind about a decision or issue in the marriage, state her thoughts and desires, but allow her husband to make the final decision, and agree to agree with it. Submission does not mean silence, nor invisibility. Nor does it not mean we are inferior. We need to speak to our husbands if we have a different opinion or view of a situation.

In a mentoring situation, a woman may need to be taught there are appropriate ways to do this and inappropriate ways to do this. We want to teach respect for husbands in all situations. In order to be submissive and speak the truth to our husbands, we need to do it with the right mindset; the right attitude, and right motives. A woman who approaches her husband to disagree publicly, in front of the children, or with angry words is not showing submission or respect. However, to teach a woman to gently approach her husband with a "have you thought about it from my perspective?" or "I am seeing this another way" approach in the quiet of their home or bedroom, with no one around to hear, would make most husbands more open and approachable.

How does a mentor teach this approach? What does a young woman, who is headstrong (just like I was when I was younger), need to learn in order to willingly and cheerfully obey God's command to submit to her husband, to speak to him with a submissive attitude of respect and love when she disagrees?

The simple answer is, "Scripture." First, we must teach who God is. In order to trust His commands we must understand His character.

I prayed to the LORD my God and made confession, saying, "O Lord, the great and awesome God, who keeps covenant and steadfast love with those who love him and keep his commandments." Daniel 9:4
The steadfast love of the LORD never ceases; his mercies never come to an end. Lamentations 3:22

When a woman understands the love behind God's commands, we can then teach His commands, including these:

- *Wives, submit to your own husbands, as to the Lord. For the husband is the head of the wife even as Christ is the head of the church, his body, and is himself its Savior. Now as the church submits to Christ, so also wives should submit in everything to their husbands.* Ephesians 5:22-24
- *Wives, submit to your husbands, as is fitting in the Lord.* Colossians 3:18

Likewise, wives, be subject to your own husbands, so that even if some do not obey the word, they may be won without a word by the conduct of their wives, when they see your respectful and pure conduct. Do not let your adorning be external-the braiding of hair and the putting on of gold jewelry, or the clothing you wear-but let your adorning be the hidden person of the heart with the imperishable beauty of a gentle and quiet spirit, which in God's sight is very precious. For this is how the holy women who hoped in God used to adorn themselves, by submitting to their own husbands, as Sarah obeyed Abraham, calling him lord. And you are her children, if you do good and do not fear anything that is frightening. 1 Peter 3:1-6

I know some will find these offensive – until they live them. One way a woman shows respect to her husband is to submit to the authority God has given him in the home. I think we would all agree the Proverbs 31 woman was submissive to her husband. She feared the Lord and God commended her for it. Verse 11 says, *The heart of her husband trusts in her, and he will have no lack of gain.*

A submissive wife draws her husband in, he trusts her and, in a healthy marriage, the husband gives her some free rein to run the home and develop her own gifts. Each one fulfills the role God has laid out, the husband subduing the earth and the wife helping in whatever way she is gifted.

Submit To The Lord

Obviously, this is not a magic trick working perfectly in every marriage. If the husband is controlling or has an otherwise skewed understanding of a wife's submission (he believes he is the hammer and she is the nail!), he may be the one who needs to be mentored. But, if a woman has been rebelling against the leadership of her husband, it may take time for him to believe she has become a submissive wife. A mentor may be able to encourage her to be patient and persevere while her husband is convinced of the change. Proverbs 31:28-29 give us the desired outcome of a submissive and respectful wife, *Her children rise up and call her blessed; her husband also, and he praises her, "Many women have done excellently, but you surpass them all."*

Ephesians 5:21-22 tell us we are to submit to each other out of reverence for Christ and to our husbands as unto the Lord. This is a command of God. The understanding we may need to help a young woman come to is the need for submission. God is not just honored when we obey but, as when we obey any of His commands, it speaks of our love and worship for Him. In John 14:23 Jesus says, *If anyone loves me, he will keep my word, and my Father will love him, and we will come to him and make our home with him.* When we submit to our husbands, we submit to the Lord.

Submission is about obedience to God in the way we respect our husbands. Our culture tells us it is a demeaning and foolish practice from another era when women were not respected or treated fairly. Sadly, some churches have interpreted this to mean that the woman has no decision making power and the man is to rule the family with an iron fist.

The truth is that God's commands about marriage are good for every marriage, when both spouses follow them. Whenever we obey God's commands we are liberated from the bondage the world would have us live in.

Right after Peter was told not to preach the Word of God in Acts 5, he was found by the civil authorities in the temple teaching the people. In verse 28 they confronted him with these words, *We strictly charged you not to teach in this name, yet here you have filled Jerusalem with your teaching, and you intend to bring this man's blood upon us.*

Peter's response to them was simple, *We must obey God rather than men.*

The command God has given us to submit to our husbands can be taught to a young woman as simply as, *We must obey God rather than man.* Though the world is losing respect for the role of a man in his family, God has made it clear he is to lead the home. (We can emphasize God's blessings of peace and joy in the home when we do things His way.) There is also an expectation of mutual love and respect in the way this leadership is accomplished within a marriage and family. The man is called to be a devoted husband, showing love and respect for his wife. God allows a wife to refuse to submit to a husband who is asking her to do something not of God, something wicked or sinful, in which case, she must obey God over her husband.

I am often amazed at how God blesses me when I submit to His authority and do things His way. Shortly after my husband and I started attending a Bible-believing church there was an announcement in the bulletin about an upcoming marriage conference. I wanted to go but it was pretty expensive and my husband flatly rejected it. I brought it up several times but he was not softening. I finally stopped asking but I prayed about it. When I still saw no softening after weeks of praying, I gave up. I left it in God's hands. I told God I knew He knew I wanted to go but obviously my husband was not willing so I wasn't even going to pray about it anymore and I didn't. This was early January, the conference was in April.

One week before the conference the organizers in the church came to us during Sunday School and asked to speak to us. They always had one scholarship each year but no one had applied for it yet, would we like it? My husband responded quickly, "We will if we can find someone to watch the kids."

I was elated. I had submitted to my husband's decision. I had not argued or gone behind his back and called the organizers. I had not asked three friends to pray, telling them how my husband was not giving me what I wanted (a bad habit I practiced at the time under the guise of bearing one another's burdens). I had done no scheming or conniving and God honored that submissive spirit!

Needless to say, the same God who provided the scholarship provided the childcare! He was teaching me that a submissive attitude was obedience He would bless.

Willingly! Cheerfully!

Also important for a mentor to teach is that outward obedience is not what God is looking for regarding submission. If it is "voluntary agreement" it needs to be lived out as agreement from the heart. A woman who "submits" by following her husband's decision on an issue but who does it with anger or a critical spirit, is not really submitting. Her heart is not in it.

Sometimes a woman really believes her husband is wrong, not in sin, just wrong (he doesn't like a piece of art she has chosen, a difference of opinion about a child attending a party or social event, etc.). Rather than focusing on her own responsibility to submit, she focuses on how wrong he is. The truth is we will not agree completely with every decision. What we must agree on is God's call for the husband to lead so he gets to make it. He is the one who will answer to God for those decisions. He does not need a wife who is already judging him.

Again, this is not to say a wife cannot express her disagreement and respectfully argue for her view. If the decision he makes is wrong, it will be as obvious to him as it is to us. She does not need to point it out or say, "I told you so." In fact, he may be more ready to listen to his wife with the next decision if she has not treated him like a child the last time.

Submission In The Difficult Marriage

Of course some men today will not be the kind, servant leader God calls them to be. If a woman is in a difficult or abusive marriage this topic may need to be addressed by her Pastor or a marriage counselor. The wife may need to speak the truth in love to her husband and make changes to protect herself and her children. A mentor may need to refer the wife to someone more qualified, preferably her pastor or a biblical counselor for more intensive help. Sometimes separation is necessary for the mental and physical health of the wife and children.

As a mentor you may be asked to come alongside a woman who is facing a husband who insists that his wife sin. He may tell her not to attend church (Hebrews 10:25), not to speak to the children about God (Deuteronomy 6:7). It may involve his insistence on her taking part in pornography or sexual sin of some sort (Ephesians 5:3), or lying about his sin to others (Ephesians 4:25). A wife must obey God rather than man (Acts 5:29). This can be very difficult for her.

The principles of submission become very difficult in an abusive marriage. These men often distort biblical submission to mean they rule with no mutual respect or "laying down of their lives for their wives." The view of these men seems to be that their wives must submit regardless of what he is asking her to do or with what attitude he is asking. They often insist on forgiveness from their wives when there has been no repentance.

Each marriage is different, so one set of "rules" is hard to make. People are quick to quote the verse that teaches that God hates divorce, but they are less likely to quote the one commanding the man not to be harsh with his wife. The Bible offers us these principles to consider for the difficult marriage (we have looked at some of them before):

- *With his mouth the godless man would destroy his neighbor, but by knowledge the righteous are delivered.* Proverbs 11:9
- *The prudent sees danger and hides himself, but the simple go on and suffer for it.* Proverbs 22:3

- *Why do you call me 'Lord, Lord,' and not do what I tell you?* Luke 6:46
- *But now you must put them all away: anger, wrath, malice, slander, and obscene talk from your mouth.* Colossians 3:8
- *Put on then, as God's chosen ones, holy and beloved, compassionate hearts, kindness, humility, meekness, and patience, bearing with one another and, if one has a complaint against another, forgiving each other; as the Lord has forgiven you, so you also must forgive.* Colossians 3:12-13

These verses apply to marriage in the same way they apply to all relationships of every Christian. The mentor's responsibility is to teach the younger woman, as James did, not just to read the Word of God, but to do what it says (James 1:25). We teach this for the same reason James stated in the same verse, *he* (she) *will be blessed in his* (her) *doing.*

If the marriage is abusive, please be willing to help the woman stand firm in her stance against violence or verbal abuse. Encourage her to speak to the leaders in her church, the police if necessary, and to seek refuge to protect herself and her children. Scripture speaks clearly of the advantages of marriage for the wife and children of a godly man. We must encourage reconciliation when possible, offer opportunities for repentance, and give the Holy Spirit time to work in the life of both partners toward reuniting the family.

You will find these women often protect their husbands, and it may be part of the mentor's ministry to point out to the wife that when these deeds of darkness are left in the dark, the situation will not improve. She needs to expose the deeds done in darkness. Ephesians 5:11 says, *Take no part in the unfruitful works of darkness, but instead expose them.*

Patience And Integrity
A mentor needs a great deal of patience. What seems like a horrific situation in the home to us may be her "normal." Being raised in similar circumstances or suffering abuse in some other way may leave her with little or no ability to resist or even identify it.

Women living in a physically or emotionally abusive marriage for many years may require a few more years to be willing and able to expose the problems in the light of day. A mentor will need to study Scripture with her, pointing out how God's word supports her taking a stand for what is right. This will help her gather the courage to face the issues in her marriage. A very fearful wife may need the emotional support of a mentor who will accompany her to speak with her Pastor or elders about the problems in the home, or to call the authorities if necessary.

I do not feel qualified to be the only one working with a woman in an abusive marriage like this to resolve marital issues. I encourage women I mentor who are being emotionally, verbally, or physically abused to seek a biblical counselor who is trained and experienced with this kind of trauma in a family. The mentor can hold their arms up in the battle–but they may need more help developing the right strategy to fight those battles.

The Sweet Side Of Submission

God's plan for submission is full of sweet surprises when a marriage is lived out according to God's plan by both partners. These surprises include submission to be our shield, our shelter, our safety, and our satisfaction.

Our joy comes from trusting God and obeying His Word. He tells us to submit, respect, use kind words, love one another, encourage, build one another up, keep our promises. All of these are biblical commands older women should be willing to teach a younger woman to apply to her marriage.

She won't just listen to our words, she will be watching how we treat our own husbands and live our own lives. Many of us may need to search our own hearts for how distorted our thinking may be so we can teach what the Word of God says about submission with integrity.

In Ephesians 5:21 Paul talks about, *submitting to one another out of reverence for Christ.* When a Christian couple truly wants to honor Christ in their marriage, this mutual submission will be a great boost for both husband and wife to use their gifts to glorify God in a family that remains focused on Him and not their individual "rights" in the marriage. Submission is a form of humility.   It may take time, but if a wife who has not been considerate and respectful of her husband, begins to obey God in submission, the marriage will be headed for a brighter future.

20
Training So The Word Of God Is Not Reviled

Train the young women...that the Word of God may not be reviled.
Titus 2:5

When I was the teaching leader for a Bible study ministry, a young woman transferred into our class from another state. She had been in a position of leadership in her previous class, so she came to us with some experience. Her previous teaching leader called me to let me know she was coming and recommended her for leadership in our class.

Because this young woman and her husband were new to the area, my husband and I invited her and her husband to come to our home for dinner. During the evening we talked and got to know each other. They asked us about movies we watched and books we had read. We talked about forms of worship and doctrinal teaching from the pulpits of our churches. It was an evening spent in fellowship with two other believers in the Lord Jesus Christ. Our kind of night.

Shortly after that evening, she and I went to lunch together. At some point she said to me, "Boy, you and your husband are the real deal!" I asked her what she meant. She explained she had met many Christians who live it on Sunday or at Bible study but she could see we lived out our Christianity every day. (I pray this is always so!) She based this opinion on one night in our home.

I do not tell you this to brag, but to point out that how we live delivers a real message about our faith, even when we do not know what we are communicating. Younger women do not only come to us for mentoring. They are watching us.

I had not felt like she and her husband were interrogating us. I had not realized she was paying attention to our conversation and asking a lot of questions to see if we were "reviling the Word of God." God's name and reputation were important to her. She was always watching how other Christians lived out their faith.

God's Purpose

In his letter to Titus, Paul instructs us that there is a reason for older women to teach and train the younger women. As younger women live out their faith we want them to physically and emotionally care for their husbands and children. But there is also a need for them to spiritually minister to their families for the sake of God's name, being true to His Word. God's Word is reviled when we claim His name but fail to live as He has taught us.

God's instructions always have a purpose. In Titus 2 He was not just giving older women something to do with their time, nor offering a younger woman a new friend without a purpose. If we were to do a study from the Scriptures about the importance God places on His name (which represents His person and reputation) we would see He is jealous for His Name, and He expects us to honor and not blaspheme His name. Understanding the importance of His name we will not use it in vain, neither in word or deed. Consider these verses about the name of God and the value He calls us to place on it.

- *You shall not take the name of the LORD your God in vain, for the LORD will not hold him guiltless who takes his name in vain.* Exodus 20:7
- *Some trust in chariots and some in horses, but we trust in the name of the LORD our God.* Psalm 20:7
- *Whoever believes in him is not condemned, but whoever does not believe is condemned already, because he has not believed in the name of the only Son of God.* John 3:18
- *..but these are written so that you may believe that Jesus is the Christ, the Son of God, and that by believing you may have life in his name.* John 20:31
- *The name of the LORD is a strong tower; the righteous man runs into it and is safe.* Proverbs 18:10
- *Therefore thus says the Lord GOD: Now I will restore the fortunes of Jacob and have mercy on the whole house of Israel, and I will be jealous for my holy name.* Ezekiel 39:25

So, I repeat, when we fail to honor God's Name, when we know what His Word says and do not do what it says, the Word of God is reviled.

More Like Christ

What does it mean to be more like Christ? Do we know enough about who He is and what His Name represents to be conformed to His image, with the help of the Holy Spirit?

Every decision we make can be made by asking whether the outcome of the decision would make me more like Christ or less like Him.

This conforming is to be the goal in our mentoring relationships, even for ourselves. Please take a minute to think about what this means. Are the things we are considering doing in our lives going to conform us more to the world or more to Christ?

Jesus, the God-man, has an image which is too big to describe. His character could be the topic of a book all by itself, but there are certain facets of it relating directly to the idea of mentoring women to grow in Christ-likeness. Let's look at three of them:

- The obedience of Jesus Christ to God the Father
- His attributes
- His relationships with other people.

I am always wowed by the picture of perfect obedience of Jesus Christ to God, His Father:

- *So Jesus said to them, "Truly, truly, I say to you, the Son can do nothing of his own accord, but only what he sees the Father doing. For whatever the Father does, that the Son does likewise."* John 5:19
- *If you keep my commandments, you will abide in my love, just as I have kept my Father's commandments and abide in his love.* John 15:10

And being found in human form, he humbled himself by becoming obedient to the point of death, even death on a cross. Philippians 2:8

When both women in the mentoring relationship agree the goal for both is to be conformed to the image of Jesus Christ, the conversation can be open to how God's commandments are being understood and followed. To be like Christ we must be obedient to God's commands, or at least have a strong desire to do so (John 5:19).

The attributes of Jesus are many and provide a great study to help us discern our own Christ-likeness, or that of a woman we mentor. The gospels are a good place to start (Matthew, Mark, Luke, or John). His attributes include speaking the truth all the time. He was compassionate. He did not show favoritism. He was truthful, bold and courageous in the face of evil people. He was obedient. He was full of grace and mercy in his treatment of others. The list goes on and on. A profitable study may be to look at His attributes with someone and then examine our own hearts and behaviors to see if we exhibit the same ones.

Also of great importance were Jesus's relationships with others. When Jesus looked on the harassed and helpless, the hungry or sick crowds, He had compassion on them and met their needs. He showed mercy on sinful people, feeding the hungry and healing the sick. He was forgiving and kind to the lost. If someone was blaspheming God He stood firm for God, speaking the truth, even to those who should have known it.

To His disciples, those closest to Him, He was especially thoughtful in His teaching and His care. They were followers and He prioritized them as we are to prioritize our brothers and sisters in the Lord.

Jesus, in all areas of life was the God-Man of integrity. He always did what was right in order to please His Father in heaven. Is this the image we are being conformed to? Is it the image we look to as our goal to point others to as they are being conformed to His image?

Serious Stuff

Mentors are teachers. I recently read an online article suggesting that the word "mentoring" is somehow offensive to the one being taught. One women's ministry has taken the word out of their vocabulary because it implies a superiority or inferiority, a knowing and a not knowing. From Titus 2 and other verses, it appears to me that

God wants the more faithful, the more mature, the older, to teach the younger.

Paul told Titus how to instruct the churches in Titus 2:1. *But as for you, teach what accords with sound doctrine.* He gave the instruction we already talked about to the women in Titus 2:3, *Older women likewise are to be reverent in behavior, not slanderers or slaves to much wine. They are to teach what is good...* In James 3:1, James gives a warning to any believer who teaches others, *Not many of you should become teachers, my brothers, for you know that we who teach will be judged with greater strictness.*

Regardless of whether the students are adults, small children, teens, or senior citizens, teaching is serious business to God. There will be frustrations. You may get angry with someone who wastes your time or who shows no regard for the Lord. There will be times when a woman you mentor gets hurt by the church or her husband and it will hurt you, too. You might start to work on a study guide with a woman and realize it's not fitting her needs. A woman may start out with zeal, but stops doing the study or showing any interest in spiritual growth. Decisions have to be made about time and compatibility. It can be hard to work with others.

There will also be great positives. Sometimes you will watch with excitement as God makes an obvious change of heart or attitude in someone you are working with. He may save her marriage as you are holding her arms up through the battle and help her see the truth of the Scriptures. He may grow you in ways you are not expecting but will find great joy as you go. You will see Him work, reminding you of verses to use in the moment or give you the ability to offer the right words of comfort or admonishment.

Just recently I had a friend in another state who became very ill, she was terminal. I wanted to go see her but I did not receive an invitation or a positive response to my request to visit. I have peace about that but I also, in my own mind, have been trying to think how I could get there anyway.

As I was doing a study with a mentee yesterday she made a general statement about the outcome of Abraham taking Hagar and sleeping with her to get the son God had promised. She sees it as a clear picture of the consequences of taking things into our own hands. My eyes were opened. God impressed on me I would be taking matters into my own hands if I get on a plane, not waiting for Him. Texts and phone calls may have to do until I see my friend in heaven.

When we get into God's Word with others, He will use it to speak to us, too. If we refuse His ways we are reviling His Word. We cannot only understand that as truth, but it is a truth we must pass on in a mentoring situation.

The blessing is that teaching others always teaches us. When everyone learns and grows in a mentoring situation the Word of God is not reviled. In fact, it is a win-win situation. God is glorified and we are edified.

Conclusion

21
Why Bother?

Why bother? Why spend our time mentoring women we barely know, taking precious hours from someone or something else, teaching doctrine considered passé in our culture, and requiring energy that would be useful elsewhere?

The answer is both simple and complicated. It relates to the growth of the Kingdom of God and the glory of the Person of God, as well as the good of the woman of God. The woman sitting across from us as we mentor is not the end of the line of our teaching, supporting, and encouraging. She is expected to pass it on to her children, to their children, and to others as she lives her life day to day. We must very intentionally teach every woman her generational responsibility to raise her children to love and fear the Lord but also to live in such a way her faith in Jesus Christ is evident to others, inside and outside of her home.

Deuteronomy 4:9 instructs, *Only take care, and keep your soul diligently, lest you forget the things that your eyes have seen, and lest they depart from your heart all the days of your life. Make them known to your children and your children's children.*

I was raised to believe that faith is a personal and private thing, not something to be talked about. I know very little of the faith of my ancestors. I didn't hear stories of how God brought salvation to anyone in previous generations until I was well into my forties. I had no idea how to look at a situation in life and see God at work rather than just some negative or positive set of circumstances.

When my son was in high school he went on a weekend retreat with the church we were attending at the time. One of the chaperones was a man in his thirties who had come to know Christ in his twenties. He told the boys about his salvation and emphasized how blessed these boys were to have parents who were teaching them about the Lord. He had known nothing of God or Christ, or the work of the Holy Spirit until after he was twenty years old. He could see the work of the Lord in hindsight, but no one had ever taught him to be looking for Him.

Obviously, we cannot know how God will use what we teach. We pray, we mentor who He leads us to, and we teach with integrity as we work diligently to set an example by the way we live. The rest of the work is up to God. He is able to do more than we can ask or imagine. We need to be faithful to do what He asks us to do in the process.

At the same time God is at work in us as we mentor. We do not know how God will grow our own faith and dependence on Him as we follow His call to come alongside another in her own desire to grow in faith, or be supported in godliness, as she faces difficulties in this life. There is also a constant work going on between God and the mentor. The one thing we know is that it will be a blessing.

The Next Steps
After reading this book, I pray your next step will be your first step to mentoring. Start with prayer. Ask God to equip you, to give you wisdom and guidance and then to identify the person He has for you to mentor.

Second, let someone know you are willing. Your Pastor or women's ministry leader may find it very helpful to know you are willing when the need arises.

Third, keep studying the Scriptures as you wait on the Lord. He may want you (as He did with me) in a training period before He sends you out to work.

Or, does your first step need to be to find a mentor who can help you grow in faith, knowledge, and understanding of the Lord? Ask God to lead you to the woman He has chosen to be a part of your life, be it ever so small a part. It is important.

Second, speak to those who might know who is willing to mentor you. Your pastor or women's ministry leader is a good place to start, unless the Lord has already drawn you to the person He has for you. Approach her, not with the instructions to mentor you, but humbly, asking her to prayerfully consider mentoring you.

When you choose someone in your church the accountability may be better because there are more opportunities to interact. Also, availability to meet may be easier while children are involved in other activities.

Be patient for the Lord's timing. He has commanded it and He will provide the right person.

His Glory, Not Ours

One year I took a door-to-door evangelism course in my church. We did our visits to the families of children who had come to our Vacation Bible School the summer before. One night we visited a woman who was a single mother of an eight-year old. She was raised in a mainline church without biblical teaching. We knocked on her door and told her where we were from. She was so excited, she could not wait to talk to us. She barely let the man doing the presentation talk. She had read the "Left Behind" series by Tim LaHaye and Jerry Jenkins and had studied the gospel explanation at the back of the books. "Is it really that simple?" was all she wanted to know. We fully explained the gospel, and she said she was ready to pray. God had already been at work.

As we did with everyone who responded so positively, we offered to do an eight week new believer's study. She could not wait. She had a weekday off every week and we started meeting at a restaurant for breakfast. We got through the first book, then a second and third study. She never came to our church but did start attending hers more frequently.

We did about six months of study almost every week. She loved it and said she could not wait to do for someone else what I was doing for her. During this time she started dating the father of her daughter again. Her daughter was nine by this time, and he had been a small part of their lives. Now, he's back courting her. He told her I was a part of a cult trying to pull her in. She cancelled one week and I have not seen her since. I called and called and called. I left messages, I sent her texts and notes but have not heard from her. I trust God will use the seed that was planted in her life during our time together.

I tell you this story for a reason. We can't go into mentoring just to serve other people or to gain some satisfaction in the gratitude of the one we serve. We may never see it. They let us down. They move, they die, they find someone or something new, they get a job and stop meeting with us, or they just refuse to take our calls.

The call to mentor is the call to serve Jesus by serving His people. If you decide you want to be mentored, do it to grow in faith, knowledge and understanding, to be spurred on to love and good works. Let your love for Jesus Christ and your gratitude for His work for you be your motivation, not for the person who mentors you. They, too, will move on, die, get a job, or find something new to do. For all of us it has to be all about Him if the work is to be successful, satisfying, and glorifying to God.

When we place our faith in Jesus Christ we do not just get saved from eternity in hell. We are called to a purpose, we become part of the Lord's army. He has a work for us to do and that work will not just satisfy our own need to do something for the Lord. When we cooperate with Him, He will use us to accomplish His plans for the world.

Understanding the way to do the work will bring honor and glory to His name. Five necessary attitudes and attributes for mentoring are:

- Loving others as God loves us, and as we love ourselves—seeking the best for and from another
- Speaking the truth so younger women can replace ungodly thinking with godly thinking.
- A gracious attitude. It may take time and effort as well as patience and perseverance to help someone come to a new and biblical understanding of her circumstances.
- Humility in action. We may be older, more spiritually mature, or more experienced in this life than those we mentor. Jesus served the "least of these" and we are called to do the same, willingly, cheerfully, and humbly.
- A desire to encourage, serve, and admonish our sisters in the Lord for their good and the glory of God.

He clearly calls us to teach: first our children, then to disciple those who place their faith in Jesus Christ, and then, more generally, older women are to teach younger women. These are commands. He blesses obedience to His commands (Deuteronomy 30:16).

Whether a woman looks for a mentor while she is in the throes of a very difficult marriage or a challenging rebellious child, or simply wants to know more about Jesus Christ, we sign up for a big responsibility when we agree to mentor. When we think back to our discussion about how Jesus so intentionally came to us in our need, so we are to go to others in their need.

I can tell you there is great satisfaction and great privilege in seeing the Lord care for someone through you. What an honor to watch God work in the life of another, and to know the blessing that comes from obeying His commands and anticipating the generational impact it will have for the women, and the God, we serve. These are worth the sacrifice of time, energy, money, even the emotion you will put into mentoring for the glory of God, the good of a sister in Christ and her children, and their children, and their children.

Made in United States
Troutdale, OR
04/17/2024

19248931R00096